The Concept of Anxiety in Søren Kierkegaard

MERCER
UNIVERSITY PRESS

Endowed by
TOM WATSON BROWN
and
THE WATSON-BROWN FOUNDATION, INC.

The Concept of Anxiety in Søren Kierkegaard

Arne Grøn

Translated by Jeanette B. L. Knox

Mercer University Press
Macon, Georgia

©Arne Grøn & Gyldendalske Boghandel, Nordisk Forlag A/S,

Copenhagen 1994. Published by agreement with Gyldendal Group

Agency

MUP/H769

© 2008 Mercer University Press
1400 Coleman Avenue
Macon, Georgia 31207
All rights reserved

First Edition.

Books published by Mercer University Press are printed on acid free
paper that meets the requirements of American National Standard for
Information Sciences—Permanence of Paper for Printed Library
Materials.

Library of Congress Cataloging-in-Publication Data

Grøn, Arne, 1952-
[Begrebet angst hos Søren Kierkegaard. English]
The concept of anxiety in Søren Kierkegaard / Arne Grøn ; translated
by Jeanette B.L. Knox. -- 1st ed.
    p. cm.
Includes bibliographical references (p.) and index.
ISBN-13: 978-0-88146-126-8 (hardback : alk. paper)
ISBN-10: 0-88146-126-1 (hardback : alk. paper)
1. Kierkegaard, Søren, 1813–1855. Begrebet angest. 2. Anxiety. I.
Title.
BT720.K543G7613 2008
233'.14—dc22
                    2008030501

Contents

Preface

"...only the one who was in anxiety finds rest."
Fear and Trembling (5, 27; 27)

Franz Kafka's letters, written in 1920, to Milena Jesenská "became the romance novel that none of his other novels were."[1] These letters often deal with anxiety as Kafka himself observes, so much so that several times he has to put the word in quotation marks. It is an anxiety for misunderstandings that love itself brings forward but also an anxiety that threatens to give the anticipated misunderstandings their own ghost-like or demonic life. At the end of the letters Kafka talks about how this anxiety can be expanded to include everything. It can become an "anxiety for the greatest as well as for the smallest," but he then adds, "This anxiety is perhaps not only anxiety, but also a longing for something that is more than anything anxiety-awakening."[2]

Søren Kierkegaard's *The Concept of Anxiety* (published 17 June 1844) is not a romance novel, but when Kierkegaard writes a treatise on anxiety it is because anxiety is more than anxiety. Although anxiety manifests itself in an ambiguous way, it reveals something that demands understanding: "Anxiety is the first reflex of possibility, a look and yet a terrible spell."[3]

The Concept of Anxiety is one of Kierkegaard's major works. It summarizes and anticipates themes that are developed in his other

---

[1] Villy Sørensen, *Kafkas Digtning*, trans. Jeanette B. L. Knox (København, 1968) 40.
[2] Franz Kafka, *Briefe an Milena*, Jeanette B. L. Knox's translation (Frankfurt am Main, 1966) 191.
[3] JP. vol. 1, 102 (Pap. X 2 A 22).

works, but not by presenting a unified perception in a well-rounded way. It has more the character of a work that constitutes a turning point: themes from earlier works (in particular *Either/Or*) are pursued in a broken way that gives a new starting point for the later works. Even though *The Concept of Anxiety* is an often unreasonably difficult book, it is worthwhile to read it as a gateway to the entire works of Kierkegaard.

In the following chapters I will provide a thematic introduction to Kierkegaard's body of work based on *The Concept of Anxiety*. In chapter 1, which in volume is already different from the others, I explore ways of thinking and major themes in *The Concept of Anxiety*, and then, in the following chapters I pursue them in other works, only to return to *The Concept of Anxiety*.

Since an introduction to Kierkegaard is also an invitation to read Kierkegaard himself, I give many text references as we go along, but I hope in a discrete way so that it does not disturb the coherent reading of the book. The text references are also extensive for another reason. When one wants to examine the major themes of Kierkegaard's work, it is important to connect these themes to the individual works in order to get a feeling for both the often complex development in the individual text and for the differences and tensions between the individual works. At the same time I have in a more discursive way tried to hold on to questions, cross referencing them with the individual works. It seems to me to be the most fruitful way in general—and maybe also in particular of reading Kierkegaard—to read the texts slowly (to quote Kierkegaard), but also freely and inquisitively.

That the following is a *thematic* introduction also creates certain limitations that should be mentioned now. In order to make the reading of Kierkegaard's own texts clear, I do not refer to the secondary literature on Kierkegaard (though I do give suggestions for further reading at the end of the book), just as I do not touch on Kierkegaard's biography, and I have kept to a minimum the references to other thinkers.

The Concept of Anxiety is a key work precisely because it is a treatise on anxiety. In short, anxiety shows that a human being is not automatically himself; in a crucial sense he must first become himself. A human being is a wondrously "constituted" being who is a problem to himself. The first part of this book (chapters 1–5) therefore deals with the central determinations in Kierkegaard's way of perceiving the human being: "synthesis," self, existence, freedom—and unfreedom. Adding this last word is important. The concept of anxiety leads us directly to the concept of freedom, but what freedom means is encircled negatively by examining forms of unfreedom. In anxiety the possibility of freedom presents itself, but in anxiety a human being also becomes unfree. Anxiety is an ambiguous power in man. Even the meaning of anxiety is ambiguous since anxiety is not just what a human being must free himself from. A human being also has to learn what it is to be in anxiety.

The second part of the book (chapters 6–9) further develops what is implied in Kierkegaard's perception of man. First and foremost the question is posed about what kind of relationship there is between self-understanding and understanding of other people. The answer is sought especially by linking Kierkegaard's concept of the single individual to his concept of the universally human, *det menneske-lige*,[4] and his understanding of the command of the Bible to "love thy neighbor." Based on this understanding, the meaning of the ethical and the religious is further defined. In the final chapter I examine the relationship between the analysis

---

[4] *Det menneske-lige* cannot be translated into English. The literal translation is the human-equally. Arne Grøn plays on the Danish concept *menneskelighed* (humanity), which consists of the word *menneske* (human) and *lighed* (equality). Trans.

of anxiety, Kierkegaard's perception of man, and his critical diagnosis of what he himself called "our time."

Anxiety is thus not an isolated issue in Kierkegaard. It opens up the question: what does it mean to be a human being? Since I have called the book a thematic introduction, there is good reason for putting emphasis on the question of Kierkegaard's perception of the human being, which connects all the different themes. Kierkegaard deals with the way one looks upon oneself and the other human being, and he thereby deals with the perception of what is human.

Even though Kierkegaard's treatise on anxiety is not a romance novel, what shines through the book, nonetheless, is that anxiety is linked to love—negatively as well as positively. A being in anxiety can close himself up within himself, but in anxiety he can also become aware of himself in such a way that he sees the relationship between himself and other human beings. It is in this regard that anxiety, in Kafka's words, is "more than anything anxiety-awakening."

A Bibliographical Note

The parenthetical references in this book are to Søren Kierkegaard, *Samlede Værker*, 3rd edition (Copenhagen: Gyldendal, 1962–1964). The first number in parentheses indicates the volume; the second number refers to page number. For instance, (15, 87) refers to volume 15, page 87. If there is only one number in parentheses, the number refers to *The Concept of Anxiety*. For instance, (137) refers to volume 6, page 137. The page reference to the English edition comes after the reference to the Danish edition, for instance, (15, 87; 22) indicates volume 15, page 87 Danish, page 22 English. All English passages refer to the Hong & Hong translation of Kierkegaard's writings by Princeton University Press, except for *The Concept of Anxiety*, which was translated by Reidar Thomte (Princeton: Princeton University Press, 1980). *Pap.* stands for Søren Kierkegaard's *Papirer*. JP stands for *Søren Kierkegaard's Journals and Papers* (the English translation of Kierkegaard's *Papirer*), edited and translated by Hong and Hong (Bloomington: Indiana University Press).

Preface to the English edition

Søren Kierkegaard (1813-1855) is a modern classic. His way of coining key themes such as existence, choice, and anxiety has helped form modern thought. Just to mention some prominent examples: The concept of existence that goes into philosophies of existence in the 20th century originates in Kierkegaard's work *Concluding Unscientific Postscript* from 1846. The notion of choice that goes into current ways of talking about choosing oneself can be traced back to the second part of *Either/Or* from 1843. The idea of taking anxiety both as a theme in its own right and as a lead to exploring what a human being is comes from his work *The Concept of Anxiety* from 1844. Kierkegaard's way of dealing with ethics and religion—as deep human concerns that we must understand from the beginning, as it were—remains a source of inspiration and a challenge at the beginning of the 21st century.

Yet, the reception of Kierkegaard's thought often takes the form of schematic interpretation. In particular, Kierkegaard is often seen as advocating a notion of subjectivity lacking a sense of the body, the social, and the world. Subjectivity then is seen as inward turning away from the world. A couple of decades ago, Kierkegaard's concern for subjectivity could even be seen as outdated. Although Kierkegaard stands out as a thinker of subjectivity, there is a need to rediscover what is implied in his thought on subjectivity.

The Concept of Anxiety in Søren Kierkegaard, first published in Danish in 1993, offers an opening move in such a rediscovery. The book serves a double purpose. First, it intends to help reading Kierkegaard's work *The Concept of Anxiety*, arguing for the critical importance of this work in his thought. Second, the book offers a thematic introduction to Kierkegaard's authorship via *The Concept of Anxiety*. It reads *The Concept of Anxiety* as a treatise on "difficult freedom" (to use a title taken from Emmanuel Levinas). The difficulty of human freedom is basically what Kierkegaard's thought is about. To be more specific, the book argues that subjectivity in Kierkegaard implies corporeality and temporality; that inwardness (in contradistinction to self-enclosing reserve) is inwardness in acting and understanding, thus in relating to the world; that self-relating and relating to others are intertwined. Furthermore, the book argues for a strong notion of history, at the interplay of personal and shared history, and for an equally strong notion of the universally human linked to Kierkegaard's category of the singular individual. In reviewing the notions of the ethical and the religious, it draws attention to the crucial distinction between first and second ethics which one or two decades ago was ignored in Kierkegaard-research.

Kierkegaard's works are not just one body of thought. Rather they embody a thinking taking form in constant variations. In order to show this, I have not taken the traditional route of Kierkegaard-reception in dealing with the issue of pseudonyms, which tends to turn the individual text into a closed universe. Instead, I have focused on the thought in context, that is the movement of thinking taking place in and between the individual texts.

Arne Grøn
Copenhagen, July 2008

CHAPTER 1

Anxiety

To Learn What It Is to Be in Anxiety

"In one of Grimm's fairy tales there is a story of a young man who goes in search of adventure in order to learn what it is to be in anxiety" (234; 155). This is how Kierkegaard, or rather Vigilius Haufniensis, begins the final chapter in *The Concept of Anxiety*. Kierkegaard was apparently in some doubt as to whom to choose as the writer, Søren Kierkegaard or Vigilius Haufniensis, because the name Vigilius Haufniensis was added fairly late in the writing process.[1] In any case, the writer reveals himself in this passage:

> We will let the adventurer pursue his journey without concerning ourselves about whether he encountered the terrible on his way. However, I will say that this is an adventure that every human being must go through—to learn to be anxious in order that he may not perish either by never having been in anxiety or by succumbing to anxiety. Whoever has learned to be anxious in the right way has learned the ultimate.

On a first reading, it sounds strange that one has to learn to be anxious. It sounds even stranger that one has to learn it the right way and that this is viewed as the ultimate. Why do we

---

[1] See *Concept of Anxiety*, *Supplement*, p. 177 (Pap. V B 42), and Pap. V B 72, 1, which has not been translated into English.

have to learn to be anxious? Isn't anxiety something from which we should want to free ourselves? What does anxiety mean when it is both that from which one should free oneself and, at the same time, that which one has to go through to be free?

Thus we have good reason to examine more closely the meaning Kierkegaard gives to anxiety. The mere fact that he attributes such great importance to anxiety, so great that he makes it the subject of a whole treatise, is in itself quite remarkable. It would appear that anxiety was an uncommon phenomenon in the psychology of the nineteenth century.[2] Certainly, it is not uncommon for the reflective modern view, but this is due not least to Kierkegaard's analysis of anxiety having left profound traces in the literature, philosophy, and psychology of the twentieth century.

The Concept of Anxiety is a turning point in Kierkegaard's writings not just by being a treatise on anxiety but by the way it regards anxiety. What interests Kierkegaard is not anxiety as an isolated state of mind but what anxiety *reveals* about being a human being. The treatise is exactly "the concept of anxiety." It is a treatise about the meaning of anxiety. While it is true that anxiety is a particular state of mind, its particularity is, to

---

[2] Kierkegaard observes that "the concept of anxiety is almost never treated in psychology" (136; 42). He later notes that Schelling in his philosophy often touches on anxiety but anxiety as "the suffering of the deity in his endeavor to create" (151 fn 1; 59 fn 1). But Schelling also uses the concept of anxiety in an almost Kierkegaardian sense as the anxiety of man, and he does this precisely in connection with the fall of man: "Anxiety for life itself forces man out of the center into which he was created" (*Of Human Freedom*, [Chicago: The Open Court Publishing Company, 1936] 59; translation by James Gutmann of *Philosophische Untersuchungen über das Wesen der menschlichen Freiheit* [1809; Frankfurt am Main, 1975] 74).

Kierkegaard, what it reveals about being a human being. Anxiety is a part of being human, but the question is how.

Times Change

In *The Concept of Anxiety* Kierkegaard focuses on a phenomenon that seems to belong to the periphery of ordinary human existence. Anxiety is not a word that one normally uses. If one uses it, the situation would have to be extraordinary. When talking about what it is to be in anxiety, we presumably mean to be afraid or to be fearful to an intense degree: anxiety "seizes you."

But even if the word "anxiety" is not common, it is perhaps used more often now than before, and usually in connection with the future. When using the term "anxiety"—as opposed to "fear"—for the future, it is because anxiety has both a more undetermined and more wide-ranging character than fear. It is an anxiety about catastrophes where life as we know it ceases to exist and maybe where even the possibility of human life disappears. An anxiety of this kind refers back to an underlying anxiety for death, like an anxiety for an impending disaster that ends your life.

There are many indications that we live in an era of anxiety. These indications are supported by the fact that anxiety became a leading theme in the literature and philosophy (not to forget psychology) of the twentieth century. Since the literature and philosophy of an epoch also interprets the present, our time seems to be characterized by an intense experience of anxiety. If we abstract from the fact that this modern self-consciousness might be blinding us to the anxiety of a previous time, then anxiety must be linked to "modern" experiences of emptiness and loss of meaning, until we reach a point where nothing has meaning.

As we shall see, Kierkegaard takes a more and more explicit stand towards the society of his time as it begins to manifest "modern" characteristics. He reveals anxiety-filled experiences of emptiness and nothingness, but he also describes more typical lifestyles of his own time. In these, one "establishes oneself" within the absence of meaning and by this process avoids being in anxiety. To be sure, the times have changed dramatically since Kierkegaard. He was not confronted, in the way that we are, with the possibility of ending the history of mankind by human-made catastrophes. Yet he is nonetheless concerned for the anxiety about the future, "anxiety about the next day, the day of annihilation" (13, 77; 77), anxiety that "is the next day." His point is that "the next day is a powerless nothing if you yourself do not give it your strength" (13, 77; 78). Even though we say that the future fills us with anxiety, we also provoke anxiety ourselves, because the future is not yet something determined. What makes us anxious is not only the future but also our preconceptions of the future: preconceptions that may make us unfree towards the day today and tomorrow. This means that a human being in this anxiety about the future strives or contends "with himself" (13, 78; 78).

To Kierkegaard anxiety is not just extraordinary. It is a fundamental in any human life. This human life is in itself extraordinary. At the same time, Kierkegaard describes "modern" ways of living that consist in making oneself "ordinary"—to avoid anxiety. In short, anxiety is fundamental but it is also possible to hide it or to try to escape it. In order to give anxiety such a complex meaning, Kierkegaard has to start out by giving the concept pregnancy. He focuses on those features that have already been mentioned: anxiety "seizes you," you become anxious, and anxiety has a far-reaching and indeterminate character. But he adds, as quoted above, that a human being in anxiety "contends with himself." In order to make the essential feature of anxiety stand out, Kierkegaard differentiates between fear and anxiety: fear applies to something specific while anxiety does not have a specific object, or rather the object of anxiety is "nothing" (136f; 41). Is this the same as saying that anxiety is without an object?

Anxiety points towards the future. Fear can of course do the same, but the future is manifested more clearly in anxiety. It is not this or that specifically but the unspecific or undetermined future. This does not mean that anxiety cannot be linked to a specific situation where one is about to do something, for instance, speaking to a large assembly or going traveling. Traveling for Franz Kafka has an almost mythical meaning. After having accepted an invitation to visit a friend in Georgental, he writes in a letter,

> Honestly speaking, I have this terrible anxiety for the trip; naturally not only for this particular trip and not merely about the trip but for any change. The bigger the change is, the bigger the anxiety, but it is only relative. If I limited myself to the tiniest changes— though life does not really allow this—then eventually changing the position of a table in my room becomes just as terrible as the trip to Georgental.... It is after all only an anxiety of death in the last or next to last analysis. And partly an anxiety for drawing the attention of the gods to me.[3]

Anxiety can become anxiety "for the greatest as well as for the smallest."

---

[3] Villy Sørensen, *Kafkas Digtning*, trans. Sinead Ladegaard Knox (København, 1968) 35.

Change can create anxiety because it sets before us a test. As a concrete example of a test, let us take an exam: taking an exam produces fear for what will happen. We can be asked an unexpected question or have an unfortunate contact with the external examiner and one's adviser.[4] But we can also be nervous about how we will react in the situation. Maybe we fear that we will become paralyzed. Even if we have prepared, it is possible that we will become nervous when we are actually in the situation. Do we talk about fear then? It is difficult to say what makes us nervous. But that which we are really relating to is how we are reacting. Maybe we even relate to a previous experience where we made ourselves nervous or where we paralyzed ourselves; it sounds strange here to talk about fearing ourselves.

The question is whether to call it anxiety, because we can say to ourselves "Don't worry, it is just an exam. Fortunately life goes on." In order for it to be anxiety, "the test" we are put to must be more difficult to define or to keep ourselves outside of. The question becomes who we are.

This is where Kierkegaard wants to take us: that the object of anxiety is "nothing" does not mean anxiety does not involve a situation. On the contrary, in anxiety we relate to our situation, but in anxiety the situation manifests itself as indeterminate. Kierkegaard compares anxiety with dizziness: you are gazing into a deep hole or an abyss that threatens to swallow you. In anxiety it is as if we have lost our footing, since the world we know loses its dependability. It seems that we are destroyed along with this world, and at the same time it seems that we are separated from it. The indeterminate nature of the situation that we discover in anxiety leads us back to ourselves; since the situation is

---

[4] Exams at university level in Denmark involve a *censor* (external examiner or outside judge) and an *eksaminator* (examiner or one's adviser). Trans.

indeterminate or unsettled, we must ourselves relate to it. In a sense, we relate to ourselves in anxiety because the question put before us is how we relate to the situation. In anxiety we can react to ourselves, so to speak, ahead of time. We relate to how we will relate.

Anxiety is connected to the way time is experienced. This is so not just in the sense that anxiety concerns the future. On a first reading, we can understand time as a course where one "now" takes over another "now." Time can also be concentrated in the moment that becomes the demarcation between the past and the future. Time changes, and only then is it possible to look for the coherence between the different moments in which time otherwise is broken down.[5]

That time changes means our situation changes in an essential way. We stand before new possibilities at the same time that something is lost. The important point to Kierkegaard is what it means to become an adult or to grow up. As the phrase indicates, to grow up does not happen overnight. It is not even sure that we will succeed, but our life does change nonetheless by more or less dramatic moments, such as changing school, moving away from home, or falling in love. To Kafka, traveling from his hometown Prague becomes a travel into another life, or maybe into his own inner life. To grow up is a kind of travel, especially for the person who leaves home. A variation of the important point could also be getting older when one should have grown up. If we return to the places of our childhood, we can have the strange experience that others have changed while

---

[5] Already in the first volume of *Either/Or*, Kierkegaard states that "anxiety always contains a reflection on time" (2, 143; 155). Anxiety is a "reflection category" (2, 143; 155), and the reflection on time is explained in that the past and the future are held up against each other: I see the future by seeing something as past.

we have become someone different. The loss we experience when losing a parent or when a friendship ends changes our lives. We also experience a change when our children grow up. They develop their own lives of which we can hope to be part.

Growing up and growing older are more than points. Growing up and growing older are ways that we experience the changing of time. Here is where anxiety can manifest itself because the changing of time can be a threat so that you can, as Kierkegaard says, "lose yourself." In anxiety we step and where we can come to see ourselves as a stranger. The ambiguous meaning of anxiety was this: it gives us the possibility of discovering ourselves as a self, but in anxiety we can also make us unfree, which means that we are not ourselves.

The problem with time is this: how will life separated by time be brought together into a coherent whole? A coherent whole means how we are coherent with ourselves. Anxiety enters here in between since it manifests the possibility that the coherence that holds us together dissolves. The changing of time is a theme in Kierkegaard's works to which he repeatedly returns. Time or change appear either as a burden or a threat. Time is the constant possibility of being dispersed, of becoming someone else. At one moment we are one way, in the next moment we are another way. But time and change are also a challenge and a possibility—to become yourself. For a human being only becomes himself by growing together with himself. Thus, Kierkegaard's analysis of anxiety indicates the central connection between anxiety, time, and being oneself.

The Human Being as a Synthesis

Investigating this connection further, we must start by looking at the kind of question on which the analysis of anxiety is based. As stated before, Kierkegaard asks what anxiety means; what is strange though is that a human being *can* be anxious. In order to feel anxiety the individual *himself* must be a relation between different elements, and in addition he must experience this relation himself. The critical difference between growing up and growing older is in the relationship between the past and the future. But we are not just this relation; we also relate to ourselves in the relation to our past (the person we were) and to our future (the person we may become).

That a human being is in and of himself a relation, Kierkegaard affirms by stating that man is a synthesis. It is precisely in *The Concept of Anxiety* that he emphasizes this determination, and he does this by creating two variations. The first one reads, "Man is a synthesis of the psychical and the physical," a synthesis that is "sustained by spirit" (137; 43. 142; 48). The second one states that man is "a synthesis of the temporal and the eternal" (173; 85). We will return to get a closer look at these two variations, but first we must find out what it means to say that man is a synthesis.

When Kierkegaard talks about a synthesis, he means that the two entities, soul and body, belong together. They are what they are, in a synthesis. They are in other words "factors" in the synthesis that is a relation between or a union of the two. However, this creates a problem. That man is a synthesis also implies that he is constituted. As stated before, we must understand that a human being is not put together of separate, individual entities. The point is elsewhere. Man is, by existing, "wondrously constituted" (9, 147; 176). Man is a strange "intermediate being," constituted of something heterogeneous, soul and body, or more precisely, the eternal and the temporal. But being constituted of something heterogeneous means that the coherence is fragile.

The synthesis-definition indicates two things: that the two factors belong together and that the coherence of what constitutes a human being is a problem. The relation between the two factors can become a misrelation, and if it does, isn't the coherence broken? Kierkegaard claims, however, that the coherence also manifests itself in the negative, in the misrelation. A passage later noted in *The Concept of Anxiety* says "man is a synthesis of psyche and body sustained by spirit, and therefore a disorganization in one shows itself in the others" (205; 122). In connection with Kierkegaard's *Sickness unto Death* (chapter 4), we will return to the awareness that factors in the synthesis also belong together in the misrelation. The misrelation is created by emphasizing one factor without the other. The factors, nonetheless, belong together, which is shown by one factor, abstracted from the other, becoming something else than it was. In the relation that becomes a misrelation, the factors are also negatively what they are.

Synthesis seems to mean two things: it is partly the relation that man is a relation also manifested negatively, and partly the coherence between the factors that first has to be actualized. In *The Concept of Anxiety*, synthesis primarily means that coherence between the factors is latent and needs to be actualized. The question is if the synthesis is "real." That the coherence is fragile and can fail to succeed means that the synthesis is not a given but is put before us as a task. In being human lies the task of getting the heterogeneous that we are to cohere.

In a condensed form this is the point of the determination of man as a synthesis. A human being is a constituted being in that his coherence or identity with himself is fragile. Consequently, it becomes a task to "cohere" with oneself.

It is evident that a task lies in the synthesis when we consider the two ways Kierkegaard formulates the synthesis.

Kierkegaard himself observes that the second formulation (man is a synthesis of the temporal and the eternal) is created differently than the first (man is a synthesis of soul and body sustained by spirit). Apparently, the third factor (spirit) is missing. However, a further analysis shows that also here a link connects the two factors: the moment as the critical moment that becomes a turning point. Thus the second formulation does not give another synthesis but it is "the expression for the first synthesis" (176; 88). "As soon as the spirit is posited, the moment is present" (176f; 88). This passage indicates that the second formulation is not a mere repetition of the first. In the second formulation time is posited as a problem, but this is only the case because spirit is also here the "third."

This demands an explanation. Kierkegaard not only talks about two links and the insurmountable contradiction or a separation of principles between them. The emphasis is on the third link that joins the factors in the synthesis; it is the third link that makes it a synthesis. The heterogeneous is held together by the individual relating to himself as soul and body, as temporal and eternal. In other words, the heterogeneous is held together in a self-relation. This is what Kierkegaard means by spirit being "the third factor."

Where is anxiety to be found in all of this? To continue the passage about learning to be in anxiety, "If a human being were a beast or an angel, he could not be in anxiety. Because he is a synthesis, he can be in anxiety" (234; 155). The implicit question is therefore what enables a human being to be anxious at all. Anxiety is possible since a human being is an "intermediate being," a constituted being. The first time the synthesis-definition appears in *The Concept of Anxiety* something similar is stated: "That anxiety makes its appearance is the pivot upon which everything turns. Man is a synthesis..." (137; 43).

In anxiety it becomes clear that we are not automatically ourselves; we have to become ourselves. This is the task we find in the synthesis-definition, that is to get what we are constituted of to cohere. Later, in *Sickness unto Death* from 1849, Anti-Climacus states that the task is to become concrete (15, 87f; 30); in *Sickness unto Death* Anti-Climacus plays on the meaning of "concrete" (Latin *concrescere*, "to grow together"): to grow together with ourselves, to heal.

We can understand the above based on the points of growing up and growing older. A human being is stretched out in the relation between the past and the future. Simply speaking the task is to unify the life that time separates into a coherent whole. The synthesis is thus a synthesis in time. But the relation can become a misrelation. The past can be so heavy that the future closes in on itself. Or, to turn it around, the possibilities for the future that we envision can become light or "fantastic."

That a human being, unlike animals and angels, can be anxious reveals that he in and of himself is a relation between something heterogeneous. He is constituted in a strange way so that he has to unify the heterogeneous elements of which he is constituted into a coherent whole. The possibility that man is, is thus a possibility that he is faced with as a task. In other words, man is not just in and of himself a relation; he is also a self-relation. This idea is expressed by the addition to the first formulation of the synthesis: man is a synthesis of soul and body sustained by spirit. The third element, spirit, is not a new factor, but is rather that which connects the factors in the synthesis. The factors are connected by the individual relating to himself as a soul and a body. An individual is a self that is put before the task of unifying the heterogeneous elements between which he is a relation into a coherent whole.

Anxiety reveals the possibility of the self relating to itself. And for Kierkegaard this is nothing less than the possibility of freedom.

The Possibility of Freedom

Several times in *The Concept of Anxiety* Kierkegaard writes directly about what "anxiety is." Anxiety is first and foremost linked to freedom, or rather its possibility—not all kinds of freedom, but *freedom*.

Shortly before stating the first synthesis-definition, Kierkegaard writes, "Anxiety is freedom's actuality as the possibility of possibility" (136; 42). It is not easy to make sense of this sentence. First we hear about freedom's actuality, then the possibility is redoubled, making it look even more distant. The reader will of course first take notice of freedom's actuality, but the sentence will then have to be read again backwards. For freedom's actuality is still just a possibility, and, furthermore, even just a possibility that is only outlined in anxiety. In other words, the anxiety that the sentence begins with further determines the possibility by which the sentence ends. It is this possibility that produces anxiety, but until now it has only manifested itself in anxiety as a possibility that makes one feel anxious in advance. At the same time, the sentence anticipates the line of thought that follows. For Kierkegaard shows that freedom, which is still just outlined as a possibility, is itself a particular possibility—the individual's possibility to be free. Later in *The Concept of Anxiety* Kierkegaard writes more straightforwardly, saying that "freedom's possibility announces itself in anxiety" (164; 74). Later still Kierkegaard looks back and defines anxiety as "freedom's disclosure to itself in possibility" (196; 111).

This last sentence may seem to make matters more complicated. But it can be interpreted another way. Anxiety means that the possibility of freedom manifests itself before something that itself is freedom. In other words, in anxiety man discovers freedom: his own freedom as a possibility.

This explanation raises the question of why anxiety appears when the possibility of freedom presents itself. Normally we regard a possibility as something positive; the more possibilities we have the better. It is, of course, crucial which possibilities we have; but other things being equal, it is an advantage to get our number of possibilities extended. There is, however, something ambiguous in the possibility of freedom by the way it manifests itself in anxiety. We ordinarily relate freedom with having possibilities. Kierkegaard does not, however, deal with the possibilities of freedom but about its possibility using the definite article. Even though it is the possibility of freedom, freedom itself is not a possibility like other possibilities. It is not a possibility we can choose or not choose. Once freedom has manifested itself as possibility, we cannot escape it.

If we have to choose between different possibilities and have not yet decided on one, clearly our situation is unsettled. However, when Kierkegaard states that freedom itself reveals itself as possibility, he also states that this possibility encompasses ourselves. We are set in a particular way in an unsettled, vague state. The situation in its indefiniteness brings us back to ourselves. The situation is ambiguous since it can develop in different and even opposite directions dependant upon the stand we take.

Consequently, we have a concept that is central to Kierkegaard's analysis of anxiety: *ambiguity*. Kierkegaard tries several times to determine what anxiety is or what is revealed in anxiety. At first anxiety was linked to freedom; now it is connected to ambiguity. After having defined anxiety as "freedom's actuality as the possibility of possibility," Kierkegaard writes that the dialectical determinations of anxiety have "the psychological ambiguity." "Anxiety is *a sympathetic antipathy* and *an antipathetic sympathy*" (136; 42).

Ambiguity already lies in the situation when that situation is vague or unsettled and demands a decision. However, the last passage states something more: anxiety is an ambiguous power. What is it that both attracts us and frightens us? So far the answer is that it is the possibility in the situation that it depends on our position. The situation is urgent by being indeterminate. That is to say we can take a stand in different ways vis-à-vis the situation. Ambiguity stems from the fact that a human being in anxiety is put before himself as a self who can relate in one way but also in another.

What evokes anxiety is that we not only can but must take a stand towards our situation, a situation that opens before us as indeterminate or unsettled. The fundamental example from before is that a new life begins in puberty, indeterminate and unsettled. We leave ourselves, we are no longer a child; and we are about to become someone different from what we were. Kierkegaard links anxiety to this fundamental experience (puberty) because in anxiety we become aware of ourselves through or to ourselves; we come to see ourselves.[6] In anxiety the self-relation appears since a redoubling happens. What is manifested in anxiety is the possibility of the self relating to itself (and relating differently), but anxiety itself is already a way of relating. In a particular sense anxiety becomes an experience

---

[6] Arne Grøn plays on the meaning of *mærkelig* and *mærke*, which is lost in the English translation. *Mærkelig* means strange and *mærke* has several meanings, among which are "to mark," "to become aware of," and "to note." Trans.

of ourselves. We see ourselves as someone who relates in anxiety. In anxiety we relate not just to a possibility in the future; we relate to the possibility for the self relating to itself differently or to becoming someone else.

That a human being can be anxious shows that he is a relation, heterogeneous with himself. But anxiety is not just a possibility; in anxiety a human being experiences himself—as a *self*. According to Kierkegaard, to be a self means being a self-relation, in the double sense that the self relates and thus relates to itself. The question then is this: is there coherence with ourselves when relating to ourselves? In anxiety we are not automatically ourselves, we first have to become ourselves. This was the idea implied in the task, that man was determined as a synthesis to grow together with himself. In relating ourselves to ourselves, Kierkegaard finds an ambiguous possibility: either to stand by ourselves (to embrace ourselves) or not to stand by ourselves (not wanting to be ourselves). We are already facing the last possibility when we do not admit that we have to choose.

Thus, the possibility of freedom is the possibility of self-relating but also the possibility of becoming ourselves, but also the possibility of becoming ourselves. This possibility has an peculiarly insistent nature that manifests itself as a task or a challenge we cannot escape since we already relate. We determine ourselves in relation to the possibility of freedom, and the decision may be that because of anxiety for the possibility of freedom we refuse to seize it.

Anxiety and Hereditary Sin

In the previous two subchapters I have outlined the meaning of anxiety by referring to different parts of *The Concept of Anxiety*. In fact, Kierkegaard starts differently. Until now I have abstracted from the framework with which he begins his analysis of anxiety.

This framework is indicated in the long subtitle of *The Concept of Anxiety*: "A Simple Psychologically Orienting Deliberation on the Dogmatic Issue of Hereditary Sin." Anxiety and hereditary sin are linked in the title of chapter 1, which is at least as long as the subtitle: "Anxiety as the Presupposition of Hereditary Sin and as Explaining Hereditary Sin Retrogressively in Terms of Its Origin." Chapter 1 then starts with the "Historical Intimations Regarding the Concept of Hereditary Sin." And the first sentence in the chapter takes the form of a question: "Is the concept of hereditary sin identical with the concept of the first sin?"

We must take notice of what is hereditary sin composed. Hereditary sin is formed by combining categories that conflict one another, a category of nature (natural inheritance) and an ethical category (guilt or sin).[7] We cannot be blamed for our natural inheritance. And what we can be blamed for, we cannot excuse by what we have inherited.

In chapter 1, Kierkegaard criticizes traditional notions of hereditary sin. He breaks apart the relationship between hereditary sin and the first sin, Adam's sin, because he asks in what sense is Adam's sin the first sin. What is the difference between Adam's first sin and every human being's first sin? "According to traditional concepts," the difference is that Adam's first sin carries sinfulness with it, whereas all later first sin presupposes sinfulness (125; 29f). But according to Kierkegaard this puts Adam outside of the human race. Kierkegaard's repeated criticism of traditional notions of hereditary sin is that they leave Adam "fantastically placed outside of history" (124; 28), "the history of the human race" (122; 25).

Kierkegaard's interest thus focuses on the concept of first sin. The first sin is not just first sin in the sense of number one

---

[7] Cf. JP. vol. 2, 1530 (Jfr. Pap. X 2 A 481).

in a series of things. If this was the case, no history would emerge from it. On the contrary, the first sin is "the nature of the quality: the first sin is the sin" (126; 30). This passage should be understood this way: "through the first sin, sin came into the world" (ibid.). On a first reading, it seems to confirm the "common" notion that with Adam's first sin, sin came into this world (128; 32). But "precisely in the same way it is true of every subsequent man's first sin, that through it sin comes into the world" (126; 30).

The underlying question is thus how sin enters the world. Kierkegaard's answer is seemingly double. All depends on the way one poses the question. If we understand the question in a way where we expect an explanation, we have misunderstood it. The answer we would get is that sin presupposes itself (127; 32). That is to say that we cannot get behind it—for the simple reason that the question concerns ourselves. How sin enters the world each individual understands for and by himself, "solely by himself" (144; 51). Thus Kierkegaard emphasizes the ethical character of the question. Each individual has a "primitive" (original) relationship to sin. If we ask about sin as if it were something foreign to us, we ask as a fool (143; 50). If we ask the question so that we forgets ourselves, we forget exactly that, ourselves. Each individual knows within himself what sin means.

Nonetheless, it is precisely through his analysis of anxiety that it appears as if Kierkegaard shows how sin enters the world. As the last outline suggests, we transgress by refusing to seize the possibility that anxiety opens up. And it is precisely in anxiety where we transgress. The central passage reads,

> Anxiety may be compared with dizziness. He whose eye happens to look down into the yawning abyss becomes dizzy. But what is the reason for this? It is just as much

in his own eye as in the abyss, for suppose he had not looked down. Hence anxiety is the dizziness of freedom, which emerges when the spirit wants to posit the synthesis and freedom looks down into its own possibility, laying hold of finiteness to support itself. Freedom succumbs in this dizziness. (152f; 61)

Kierkegaard compares anxiety to dizziness and attributes anxiety to the dizziness of freedom. Just as a person who looks into an abyss becomes dizzy, so freedom is now looking at its own possibility. That is to say that we suddenly discover the possibility for self-relating, but also that we must be accountable for the way we relate. It is, however, important how we discover this possibility. We discover it in anxiety by already relating to the possibility. That which anxiety manifests is thus that we cannot escape ourselves as somebody who relates even if we can try. Anxiety is not only discovering the possibility of freedom; anxiety also becomes anxiety for this possibility. And in this anxiety or the dizziness of freedom, "freedom succumbs."

This explanation of the fall of man is, in the words of Kierkegaard, psychological, but it is an explanation that resists being an explanation. Just after the previous passage, he writes, "further than this, psychology cannot and will not go" (153; 61). The explanation ends here. The important thing is a step that the single individual takes himself. The passage continues, "In that very moment everything is changed, and freedom, when it again rises, sees that it is guilty. Between these two moments lies the leap, which no science has explained and which no science can explain" (153; 61). The first sin is a qualitative determination. "The new quality appears with the first, with the leap, with the suddenness of the enigmatic" (126; 30). So, it is also through the analysis of anxiety we get back to seeing that sin enters the world by "the qualitative leap" (140; 47).

It can be difficult to get an overview of and maybe especially hard to penetrate Kierkegaard's opening discussion of the relationship between anxiety, sin, and hereditary sin. But gradually a somewhat simple answer seems to emerge, that is, Kierkegaard distinguishes between sin and sinfulness. Sin enters the world by the qualitative leap of the individual. Sinfulness, as the constant possibility of sin, is carried on through every generation. It has its history, but this history moves in quantitative categories (140; 47). However accumulated the possibility or predisposition for sin is in the history of man, sin is not caused by this. Sin is a step that the single individual has to take himself.

We started out with the meaning Kierkegaard attributed to anxiety; the question now is why Kierkegaard attributes such a central role to anxiety in connection to hereditary sin. The psychological explanation asks, what precedes sin? Even though it gives an answer, it does not explain sin. To be sure, sin enters the world *in* anxiety, but it occurs *through* a leap. However, anxiety does not simply belong to one or the other side in the distinction between sinfulness and sin. On a first reading, it seems to fall under the sinfulness that precedes sin. However, anxiety is subjectively different in that it is the single individual's anxiety almost as sin is the single individual's sin. Anxiety is a kind of intermediate term, and its meaning as intermediate term concerns the problem that is implied in the concept of hereditary sin (*arve-synd*).[8]

---

[8] *Arve-synd* is translated with hereditary sin and not original sin in the translation of *The Concept of Anxiety* by Reidar Thomte. Hereditary sin is the literal translation of *arve-synd*. Trans.

This problem concerns the relationship between the individual's natural inheritance and his actions (guilt and sin). Following the central passage about anxiety as the dizziness of freedom, Kierkegaard writes, "

> He who becomes guilty in anxiety becomes as ambiguously guilty as it is possible to become. Anxiety is a feminine weakness in which freedom faints. Psychologically speaking, the fall into sin always takes place in weakness. But anxiety is of all things the most selfish, and no concrete expression of freedom is as selfish as the possibility of every concretion. This again is the over-whelming factor that determines the individual's ambiguous relation, sympathetic and antipathetic. (153; 61)

The ambiguity of anxiety now relates to question of guilt. Anxiety does not just manifest the possibility of freedom; freedom can "succumb" in anxiety. This sounds as if freedom is something that happens to us. We become dizzy and tired, but at the same time, we give in or transgress. It is here that Kierkegaard defines anxiety as being an ambiguous power. He who becomes guilty through anxiety "is indeed innocent, for it was not he himself but anxiety, a foreign power, that laid hold of him, a power that he did not love but about which he was anxious...nevertheless loved even as he feared it." Kierkegaard adds, "there is nothing in the world more ambiguous" (137; 43). Kierkegaard attributes a central role to anxiety, founded on the ambiguity of anxiety, in connection to the problem of hereditary sin. What evokes anxiety is already ambiguous, "the abyss" or "the eye" (to stay in Kierkegaard's comparison of anxiety and dizziness). We experience anxiety by looking into an abyss, but we are "staring" into it in a fixated manner. Anxiety is a foreign power in man; it is something that overwhelms us or seizes us, but at the same time we relate in anxiety. We do something to ourselves in anxiety; we transgress. We are dealing with an ambiguity "in which the individual becomes both guilty and innocent. In the impotence of anxiety, the individual succumbs, and precisely for that reason he is both guilty and innocent" (163; 73). The impotence of anxiety does not explain *that* sin enters the world. To be sure, sin happens *in* anxiety *but* through "the qualitative leap" (147; 54).

Thus anxiety is an "intermediate term," a determination between possibility (sinfulness) and reality (sin). It is not automatically freedom; we do not decide to be anxious. Rather we *become* anxious, but at the same time anxiety is a way of relating, we feel anxious. Anxiety is an "entangled freedom, where freedom is not free in itself" (143; 49). That sin enters the world in anxiety means that it is not caused by a free, arbitrary decision, nor is it out of necessity.

Thus the ambiguity of anxiety occurs when anxiety "happens" to us but, at the same time, we "ourselves" are anxious since we relate to ourselves in anxiety. By virtue of this ambiguity, anxiety gives us the possibility of discovering ourselves. When we become self-conscious, something critical happens to us. At the same time that it "happens" to us, it happens "by" our own doing because we become conscious of ourselves. However many other people put pressure on the individual, we are dealing with an experience that we must go through ourselves.

Innocence and Anxiety

"But innocence is lost only by guilt. Every man loses innocence essentially in the same way that Adam lost it" (131; 36). The individual's first sin is just as original as the first sin, the fall of man. There is good reason to examine what the fall of man means in the life of an individual. What happens to the individual when sin enters the world by its qualitative leap? Kierkegaard himself initiates an examination of the innocence that precedes the fall. Innocence is also in each individual's life as original as the innocence that precedes the fall.

First, Kierkegaard warns against confusing innocence and immediacy (130; 35). It may not be all that evident why he does so. His warning is stated with the motto that we must begin by forgetting what Hegel has discovered. But his disagreement with Hegel serves a purpose. Kierkegaard's point is that innocence is not something that should just be annulled, which is exactly what Hegel is doing to immediacy. Innocence is *something* (Kierkegaard's italics); it "is a quality, it is a *state* that may very well endure." It is "not an imperfection in which one cannot remain, for it is always sufficient unto itself" (132; 37).

Kierkegaard's meaning becomes clear when we understand innocence as the innocence of childhood. Innocence is not just that which comes before puberty. It not only finds its meaning from that which is going to come after, but it is something in and of itself. It is not something imperfect that has to be evaluated on its deficiency. On the contrary, it has a perfection of its own, a peculiar perfection or well-roundedness that is in balance with itself. But childhood has an understanding, including an understanding of adult life. This Kierkegaard implies by returning to anxiety. Even though childhood innocence is self-sufficient, it is also directed towards something other than itself.

Regarding anxiety in innocence, Kierkegaard says briefly, "In observing children, one will discover this anxiety intimated more particularly as a seeking for the adventurous, the monstrous, and the enigmatic" (136; 42). A child has a sense of what is to come. Childhood is in and of itself not a homogeneous phase but is characterized by changes to which the child himself relates. An example of this process is becoming three years of age. Before a child reaches three, she can circle around what it means to become three. When the child becomes three, he or she is a big person. The child starts to attend kindergarten, stops using the pacifier and diapers. Becoming three can appear as something almost magical. When the step from day care to kindergarten is made, the child also goes through this changed experience in play. He or she pretends time and time again that a doll or the parents are the child who has to be brought and fetched from the kindergarten. The older child is more and more preoccupied by adult life and by what is to come. When playing enigmatic and adventurous games, the child puts himself in relation to this other life.

According to Kierkegaard, it is precisely in relation to adult life that innocence means ignorance. How can innocence be both ignorance and anxiety anticipating an ambiguous possibility? That this ignorance is not just the absence of knowledge remains in force. It is partly a specific ignorance, an ignorance about what is still not there, the sexual (which itself entails a consciousness, as we shall see). And innocence is partly "a knowledge that denotes ignorance" (159; 68). This knowledge in ignorance is modesty. It is a knowledge that there are two sexes, but not a knowledge that consists in relating to this difference. The anxiety of modesty is ambiguous. "There is no trace of sensuous lust, and yet there is a sense of shame. Shame of what? Of nothing. And yet the individual may die of shame. A wounded modesty is the deepest pain, because it is the most inexplicable of all" (ibid.).

Modesty is thus understood by Kierkegaard within the framework set by innocence. Or rather, modesty is not automati-

cally innocence, but it is trying to maintain or hold on to innocence at the same time as it is a knowledge about the difference
in sex. When the individual feels the anxiety of modesty, he
shies away from or evades the understanding that he is
determined as a particular sex (159ff; 68ff). We protect ourselves
from that which threatens our immediate unity with ourselves.

It is somewhat of a puzzle that Kierkegaard limits modesty
in this way to a maintained innocence, a "border" innocence.
Thus the phenomenon seems to be restricted on both sides,
both in relation to the child before and the adult after. A child's
sense of modesty can be offended, and consequently he can feel
shame. Modesty and shame are also phenomena that belong to
adult life. Maybe modesty is the adult's ability to maintain the
connection to his childhood and puberty. But by finding an
anxiety of modesty within innocence (meaning "a knowledge that
denotes ignorance"), Kierkegaard once again states that
innocence maintains its own peculiar knowledge. Innocence
itself is already a way of relating to that difference that marks
adult life.

There is at least one more problem in Kierkegaard's
description of innocence. Kierkegaard writes that innocence is a
state of mind that can last. To this we must object that innocence
also holds a knowledge of the life to come and thus a knowledge
that it does not last in and of itself. Kierkegaard's claim that
innocence can last in and of itself must mean that innocence, as
mentioned, makes up its own world that is not automatically
replaced by another. Even though we talk about the child having
to grow and become an adult, innocence is not dissolved in a
smooth and natural transition. Innocence is lost enigmatically
and suddenly through a leap. Of course, a "leap" also occurs
during childhood. A child can find himself set apart from himself
by feeling that he is no longer what he used to be. He will get a

different awareness of himself. Since Kierkegaard talks about the leap using the definite article, the individual's qualitative leap, it must then have an additional meaning.

In order to understand this additional meaning we have to look at what he writes about the spirit in innocence. "In innocence, man is not qualified as spirit but is psychically qualified in immediate unity with his natural condition" (135; 41). That such an "immediate" entity could be implied in innocence does not seem to fit in with what we have just heard. Innocence is a world in itself in virtue of its being a particular way of relating, precisely to the limits of this world. Thus it is insufficient to state that in innocence man is not determined as spirit. Kierkegaard does in fact add that "the spirit in man is dreaming" (ibid.). Or, as he writes a little later, "so spirit is present, but as immediate, as dreaming" (137; 43). But by being present anyhow the spirit disturbs the immediate unity between the soul and the body. As we saw earlier, the spirit has to be understood as the third that joins the two factors by the individual relating to himself as a soul and a body. In other words, the spirit means the self-relation or the connection in the self-relation. The spirit is present as dreaming in innocence since the child relates to the coming possibility through which he will change. Kierkegaard calls the spirit in this case an ambiguous power; it is hostile insofar as it disturbs the immediate coherence but friendly since the possibility for change that it contains is to become oneself (again). That the spirit is present as dreaming means that the individual is relating to himself since he senses the contour of another life to come without taking it as a possibility for himself. In Kierkegaard's formulation, the spirit relates itself to itself since it relates as anxiety (138; 44).

This anxiety means that man in innocence can become disturbed by himself. "Only a word is required" (138; 44), and anxiety has something to work on. Kierkegaard refers to God's words to Adam: "But of the tree of the knowledge of good and evil, thou shalt not eat of it" (Genesis 2:17). He adds, "the prohibition induces in him anxiety, for the prohibition awakens in him freedom's possibility. What passed by innocence as the nothing of anxiety has now entered into Adam, and here again it is a nothing—the anxious possibility of being *able*" (138; 44). In this anxiety, innocence is brought "to its uttermost" (139; 45). Even though we cannot speak of a natural transition from innocence, an intensification, nevertheless, takes place.

In what then does the additional meaning consist when Kierkegaard speaks not only about a leap, but *the* leap? Here a leap means that the individual is changed by the consciousness of himself. The change consists in that the individual now becomes conscious of himself, as a self. In other words, the self-relation emerges. The spirit is no longer dreaming but is breaking through.

Sexuality and History

After having traveled this long road, we are now back to the determination of man as a synthesis. Kierkegaard observes that in innocence there is an immediate unity between the soul and the body, but that this synthesis is not actual. For "the combining factor is precisely the spirit, and as yet this is not posited as spirit" (142; 49). That the spirit is "posited as spirit" means that the individual becomes conscious of himself as a self who has to connect the factors in the synthesis.

But, if it is to be a task to connect the factors, they first have to be separated. "In the moment the spirit posits itself, it posits the synthesis, but in order to posit the synthesis it must first pervade it differentiatingly, and the ultimate point of the sensuous is precisely the sexual" (ibid.). With the fall of man the individual becomes estranged from himself by being separated out from himself. This means that the factors are separated since the difference between them is made into a contradiction by accentuating to its "uttermost" one factor, corporality or sensuousness, in relation to the other factor. Thus the spirit seems to step over to the other side so that the relation becomes a relation between sensuousness on one side and spirit on the other. Later on in *The Concept of Anxiety* we read that the sexual is an expression of the immense contradiction, "that the immortal spirit is determined as *genus*" (160; 69). The other synthesis-definition is outlined here—the synthesis between the eternal and the temporal.

The spirit does not, however, cease being "the third." On the contrary, the spirit or the self manifests itself now as the third that joins the factors of the synthesis. Implicit in the previous passage is that the spirit (or the individual as a self) is determined as gender, sex. In puberty the individual has the strange experience of being determined by his sex. The individual becomes aware of himself, but he also encounters himself as a self. He discovers himself as being a self by stepping out of himself and thus determined by his sex. The task implicit in the synthesis is manifested, to unify the heterogeneous into a coherent whole. "First in sexuality is the synthesis posited as a contradiction, but like every contradiction it is also a task, the history of which begins at the same moment" (142; 49).

I will go further into this passage both now and in chapter 6. The sexual, as we have already seen, exists in modesty where there is knowledge of the difference as determined by sex, but this is not a knowledge that even lies in the fact of relating to such a difference. That is to say that the sex drive as such is not present (159; 68). In a sense the sexual is not yet posited. This means that in the sexual there is a knowledge or a consciousness:

the self-consciousness of the individual as determined by the difference in sex. When the sexual becomes conscious (158; 67), the individual understands himself differently. This difference sets in such a way that the individual cannot go back behind this consciousness.

It is worth noticing the way sexuality and history are linked together in the previous passage. Prior to this passage Kierkegaard explicitly states that "without sexuality, no history" (142; 49). "No angel has a history," Kierkegaard states at least twice (130; 34. 142; 49). Since a human being is heterogeneous with himself, he is put before the task of determining himself in relation to himself. In this way an individual will have a history.

Kierkegaard's reflections in *The Concept of Anxiety* are particularly focused on what it means that a human being has a history. I have already hinted at this point a couple of times. When Kierkegaard takes a position on the traditional perceptions of hereditary sin, it is in and of itself an argument against these perceptions that they place Adam outside of history. A shared human history exists in virtue of the fact that every man is separated as a single individual. The underlying question is what it takes for an individual to have a history. Kierkegaard's indirect answer is that the individual is born into a historic context, a "nexus" (163; 73) of history, but that he will only have a history by virtue of a "transcendence" (143; 50), namely through his qualitative leap that is not a part of the historic context. In order to have a history the individual must have a starting point or a critical moment through which he views history. When Kierkegaard here talks of the moment, it is not meant as a particular event in the life of a human being. It is the break that happens when a human being becomes self-conscious. This break can be linked to a particular event or, even more plausible, a series of events. An individual's "becoming self-conscious" has in a sense its own history, but the individual only sees this history in retrospect *after* he has reached self-consciousness. Even though a chain of events appears in retrospect, Kierkegaard can write of the critical "moment" because merely becoming self-conscious *is* a break, an awakening. A demarcation line is created between before and after so that a history can be told. It is only by virtue of this critical, awakening "moment" that in retrospect we can attribute crucial meaning to particular events. To become self-conscious means that there is a difference set upon ourselves: we have become different from what we were before. We become a self to ourselves. Any step backwards will be taken with this self-consciousness. In this sense we cannot go behind the moment that has awakened us. We can go back by remembering our own history, but this means we see this history from the perspective of self-consciousness.

To become self-conscious is not a one-time event, nor is it a one-time event of the future. Even though we have become self-conscious in the sense that innocence is lost, we can become unclear about ourselves. Our self-consciousness can shift so that we think we only now become self-conscious, but it is precisely because of this self-consciousness that our history changes. This confirms the conclusion we have just reached that in order to have a history a human being must have himself or self-consciousness as his point from which to depart.

In *The Concept of Anxiety* Kierkegaard links anxiety and the moment by saying that "in the individual life, anxiety is the moment" (170; 81). Here we are dealing with anxiety in its fullest sense wherein the individual becomes aware of himself in anxiety. This moment is linked to the first sin or the Fall. If the first sin was just sin number one in a chain of sins, there would not be any history. A link exists between sexuality and history that was shown in a previous passage; history begins "at that same moment" when the synthesis is posited as a contradiction and task (142; 49).

Why is sin so important? Sin is not just a person doing something morally wrong every now and then, because, in that case, we only have a more or less loose series of separate acts. It is true that to sin is to err or to transgress, but sin is fundamental by the position we take towards it, since we are seeking our own. What is essential is that man is "marked" by sin as he realizes that he cannot escape himself. We discover that we have already erred and thus we tie ourselves down. The question is what we are going to do about ourselves as someone who has already started off on the wrong foot. Since we are already "marked" by ourselves, we have a history.

Thus, the individual has no history of his own until the moment that awakes him. But a further point, to which Kierkegaard only alludes, is that an individual's history has a beginning that precedes this awakening, and that beginning is innocence. If we wish to tell our personal history, it is not only the chronology beginning with childhood. It is in relation to and based on childhood that the later personal history can be told. In childhood an individual is brought into the world. It is this world from which the individual separates himself when he is no longer a child. But it is also this world through which he has originally experienced himself, and to which a later world therefore has to be related. Childhood, being the beginning of an existence, evades the backward glance of self-consciousness at the same time that the individual, more or less successfully, carries along the experiences of childhood. Childhood is as a world apart, lost when it is remembered, but in order to have a personal history it is necessary to remember it.

However, Kierkegaard's further reflections in *The Concept of Anxiety* go in a different direction. In order to discover this we must look at the structure of the book. The title of his chapter 1 links anxiety and hereditary sin. Until now we have been examining the anxiety before the fall of man (the anxiety of innocence, the anxiety of modesty) and the anxiety in which the fall takes place. It would be natural to ask about anxiety after the fall. But Kierkegaard does not address this question until chapter 4. What about chapters 2 and 3 then? I have already quoted from them heavily in the previous chapters of this book. Kierkegaard himself notices somewhere that what he is writing in chapters 2 and 3 could have been placed in chapter 1 (180 note 2; 93 the note). But chapters 2 and 3 surely must say something that goes beyond chapter 1.

Chapter 2 has the title "Anxiety as Explaining Hereditary Sin Progressively," and here Kierkegaard informs us of where we are in his reflections on the concept of anxiety. The task is "to immerse oneself psychologically in the state that precedes sin and, psychologically speaking, predisposes more or less to sin" (166; 76), but at the same time we now find ourselves after Adam's sin. However, a state of innocence must also exist in subsequent man (145; 52). The difference is that anxiety changes in the subsequent individual. Anxiety becomes more reflective because the individual participates in the history of mankind. This history, which is also the history of the individual, speaks of sin and guilt. When the individual relates to the history from which he originates, it is a history in which anxiety can reflect itself. That anxiety in the subsequent individual is more reflective "may be expressed by saying that the nothing that is the object of anxiety becomes, as it were, more and more a something." Kierkegaard is quick to add, "We do not say that it actually becomes a something or actually signifies something. ...For what holds true of the innocence of the subsequent individual also holds true of Adam" (153; 61). It is only "as it were" that the object of anxiety turns into something. Even though the history of mankind predisposes man to sin, sin is also posited by the qualitative leap taken by the subsequent individual. "The subsequent individual has a 'more' in relation to Adam, and again a more or a less in relation to other individuals. Nevertheless, it remains true that the object of anxiety is a nothing" (166; 77). This was the answer outlined earlier when Kierkegaard distinctly differentiated between sinfulness that moves in qualitative determinations and sin that is a new quality. Just as sinfulness (the possibility or the predisposition of sin) rises or falls throughout history, so does anxiety (145; 52).

Indirectly the question being asked in chapter 2 is what is the meaning of the history of mankind for the individual? The meaning is manifested in anxiety. The sinfulness that the individual inherits is carried in anxiety. The title of the chapter even identifies anxiety with hereditary sin (anxiety as hereditary sin). That anxiety is reflected in the history of the race is a predisposition for sin (153; 62).

What is then "the something that the nothing of anxiety may signify in the subsequent individual," and what is hereditary sin in the strict sense (153; 62)? As sensuousness increases in the history of the generation, so anxiety increases too. This is explained in what we were told a moment ago. "If in one part of the synthesis there is a 'more,' a consequence will be that when the spirit posits itself the cleft becomes deeper and that in freedom's possibility anxiety will find a greater scope" (155; 64). The meaning of sensuousness is expanded to include sexuality. Kierkegaard now emphasizes that sensuousness is not sinfulness, as such the sexual is not the sinful. Sin is a leap that the individual takes himself. Since sin is posited it *makes* sensuousness sinfulness (166; 76).

In a sense the structure of *The Concept of Anxiety* is clear once again; one thing is the history of mankind that always moves in quantitative determinations (129; 33); another thing is the qualitative leap of the individual. And yet history indicates that anxiety increases to such an extent that its object "as it were" becomes something. The terrible possibility that "*anxiety about sin produces sin*" (163; 73) is even outlined as a "maximum" (146; 53). Here anxiety becomes what it will be later on: the anxiety of sin. Until now anxiety has only anticipated the possibility of sin, but not its actuality. The beginning of chapter 1 states explicitly that the reflective anxiety of the subsequent individual is not, however, "anxiety about sin, for as yet the distinction between good and evil is not, because this distinction first comes about with the actuality of freedom" (145; 52).

Thus the indirect question in chapter 2 is, what does history mean for the individual's anxiety? Chapter 3 repeats the question about the meaning of history but from a different angle. The title of this chapter is "Anxiety as the Consequence of that Sin which Is Absence of the Consciousness of Sin." In a certain sense the chapter unfolds as a historical-philosophical reflection. That which Kierkegaard has stated so far presupposes a historical context, namely Christianity. In this chapter he indicates the Christian historical context by showing the meaning of the moment for history. In short he says that "only with the moment does history begin." The moment is determined as "that ambiguity in which time and eternity touch each other, and with this the concept of *temporality* is posited" (177; 89). Kierkegaard refers to that around which everything in Christianity circles, the fullness of time, where the moment as the eternal includes history. To Kierkegaard the alternative to Christianity is first and foremost "Greek culture," but what classical Greek philosophy misses is precisely the concept of the moment and temporality that, to Kierkegaard, is due to its not having a concept of the spirit (176ff; 88ff).

Kierkegaard attributes a universal meaning to anxiety. In a certain way anxiety is part of being an individual. But the analysis of anxiety hinges on the understanding of sin as the step by which the individual is marked. The question is, what happens when the consciousness of sin is missing or fails to appear? In chapter 3 Kierkegaard wants to show that anxiety manifests itself nonetheless. It manifests itself in the paganism of an individual's ambiguous relation to destiny. In Judaism guilt is emphasized so that the individual does not seem to be distinguished from mankind, but the relation to guilt is even more ambiguous. It is true though that guilt in a very definite way does seem to be "something." It is so definite that guilt is what the individual fears but, "while anxiety fears, it maintains a subtle communication with its object." Life presents us with "sufficient phenomena in which the individual in anxiety gazes almost desirously at guilt and yet fears it" (189; 103).

With this Kierkegaard has given more than a historic outline, as he states himself "what has been indicated briefly here about the relation of the world-historical is repeated within Christianity in the individualities" (190; 104).

Before giving his historic outline, Kierkegaard says that not reaching sin is, in the deepest sense, a sin (181; 94). On a first reading this can be difficult to understand. But the meaning must be this: to reach sin "in the deepest sense" is to reach a consciousness of sin (as that which the individual is distinguished as). In this we state that sin can very well exist even though a consciousness of sin in the strict sense is missing. Kierkegaard observes that the historic absence of consciousness of sin is not the state of innocence. That which is missing is the understanding that consciousness of sin provides: the understanding that a human being is determined to become a spirit or a self.

A more radical possibility is that even though this understanding has entered history, it can be lost again. This is what Kierkegaard means by "spiritlessness." He distinguishes between the absence of spirit (182; 95) where the concept of spirit is missing, and spiritlessness where the understanding has been lost. The first characterizes paganism while the last is a possibility within Christianity (182; 95). The concept of spiritlessness becomes a key for Kierkegaard's diagnosis of his own time. More about this later.

Anxiety about Evil—and Anxiety about the Good

So far in *The Concept of Anxiety* Kierkegaard has focused on anxiety "before the fall of man" (the anxiety of innocence, the anxiety of modesty) and the anxiety in which the Fall takes place (anxiety as the dizziness of freedom) as well as the change that happens with anxiety over the course of history (the reflected anxiety). Even though guilt accumulates over the course of history so that in the end it is as if "the guilt of the whole world" unites to make the individual guilty (194; 109), it is still true to say that every individual becomes guilty only through himself (146; 53). To complete the circle Kierkegaard explains that "just as Adam lost innocence by guilt, so every man loses it in the same way" (130f; 35).

At this point the question naturally arises: what about anxiety "after the fall of man"? Kierkegaard does not take up the question until chapter 4. The title of the chapter is "Anxiety of Sin or Anxiety as the Consequence of Sin in the Single Individual." Kierkegaard begins this chapter by indicating a change in the examination of the meaning of anxiety. As previously noted, anxiety was described this way: the possibility of freedom reveals itself to the individual as an ambiguous possibility, which is exactly what makes one feel anxious. And in anxiety *for* the possibility of freedom the individual transgresses. Then when the individual has taken the qualitative leap, we may think that anxiety would disappear, because anxiety concerns the mere possibility. But the reality that is posited by sin is "an unwarranted actuality" (196; 111). As such, it should not continue. Thus, anxiety "comes into relation with what is posited as well as with the future." The question is how we deal with this reality (the "posited") and what will become of it in the future ("the future"). However, a crucial change has occurred, for "this time the object of anxiety is a determinate something and its nothing is an actual something, because the distinction between good and evil is posited in concreto" (196f; 111f).

This summarizes the first passage of chapter 4. Within this central chapter an ascending movement is again outlined as Kierkegaard distinguishes between anxiety about evil and anxiety about the good. Anxiety returns "again" after the Fall, but it has changed appearance. Kierkegaard observes that anxiety has lost "its dialectical ambiguity" since it now relates to a given difference, the difference between good and evil (197; 112). The matter is, however, not that simple. The upward movement described in chapter 4 intensifies the ambiguity of anxiety.

Now the individual in the Fall has personal knowledge of the difference between good and evil. The individual himself is determined or "marked" by this knowledge since it is a knowledge about what he should do in relation to what he has already done. The question is, what position will the individual take regarding his past? For the individual to understand what he should do, he must understand what he has done. The relationship between past, present, and future is presented as an ethical-existential problem. The synthesis in time becomes an ethical matter.

Since the difference between good and evil is a turning point, it is natural to distinguish between anxiety about the good and anxiety about evil. But why not just focus on anxiety about evil? The question is, in fact, why anxiety about evil? For repentance should succeed anxiety. Kierkegaard has previously pointed out that a person cannot be anxious but only repentant of a past offense if indeed it is actually past (179; 91f). "As soon as guilt is posited, anxiety is gone, and repentance is there" (189; 103). But repentance will reveal itself to be an ambiguous phenomenon that leaves a door open to anxiety.

The problem is how to free ourselves from a past that is buried in guilt. We can free ourselves, by not repeating the past, that is to say by becoming free "forwardly." But here anxiety anticipates the possibility of failure. "Anxiety is ahead; it discovers the consequence before it comes, just as one feels in one's bones that a storm is approaching. The consequence comes closer; the individual trembles like a horse that gasps as it comes to a halt at the place where once it had been frightened" (200; 115). When we realize that we have failed we can be anxious of failing again. We can be anxious of being weak or of making ourselves weak. What we repent and what also makes us anxious can, in Kierkegaard's words, have as much to do with "addiction to drink, to opium, or to debauchery, etc." as with "pride, vanity, wrath, hatred, defiance, cunning, envy, etc." (ibid.). Provided that we repent this anxiety about evil can be said to be "in the good" (203; 119). We react against the possibility of evil. But why then talk about anxiety? How does ambiguity enter in relation to the good that we want? In repentance we should become free of a past buried in guilt, but the question is, how does repentance free us? To be free demands that we must acknowledge that we have failed, but if we see our guilt, will it then not become impossible to free ourselves of the past? Repentance is of course necessary. For if we do not acknowledge the past, it will tie us down even more. By repenting the individual seeks to overcome the past so as not to repeat it, but is repentance stopped by itself? In repentance the required act is postponed or delayed (202; 117-18). Thus a new guilt appears that demands a new repentance.

It makes sense to talk of anxiety about evil. The ambiguity of this anxiety consists in this: even though we react against the possibility of repeating what we know is wrong, we are, at the same time, unsure about ourselves. In anxiety we can stare at guilt. The possibility from which we distance ourselves also attracts us at the same time. Even repenting the evil we have done is ethically ambiguous. It is required that we repent, but repentance is always one step behind; it comes too late and moreover delays the act that ethics demands.

The question then is why it is not enough to have anxiety about evil. Why also have anxiety about the good? What kind of anxiety is anxiety about the good, and what does this good consist of that makes us anxious? Kierkegaard states briefly that the good cannot be defined at all, only to claim in the next sentence that "the good is freedom" (196 note; 111 the note). But with this statement, Kierkegaard does not tie down the good to a particular content. The good is "the restoration of freedom, redemption, salvation" (203; 119). Thus anxiety about the good means that we resist being free or being ourselves. This needs an explanation, for why should we react against this possibility that presumably is something every human being is striving to actualize? In anxiety about the good, we are dealing with a more intense resistance than in the anxiety for the possibility of freedom. We do not just find ourselves in a vague, unsettled state where we must make a choice; on the contrary, our state is settled. The resistance consists in that we keep ourselves in an unfree state. In order to understand why this is so, we must go back a little.

Becoming ourselves means achieving coherence or continuity in our lives. It is, however, not just the problem of unifying different periods of our lives into a coherent whole. The problem is intensified when we refuse to acknowledge something. Anxiety about evil showed that the attempt in "getting ourselves back" through repentance fails. Now Kierkegaard furthermore introduces an unwillingness "to become whole." Here the good—the restoration—demands a form of loss of self. What has to be gotten back is precisely what we hide from ourselves. We must allow ourselves to be interpenetrated, that is to say, we must give up our unwillingness. Insofar as we put up a resistance we must be redeemed from the outside. We must be given or told about the coherence with ourselves. In anxiety about the good the resistance is intensified by asserting ourselves against freedom as a possibility coming from the outside. This is, however, a self-assertion that, at the same time, means an intensified fragmentation. The ambiguity of anxiety increases here, since the individual closes himself to the possibility of good while at the same time being affected by it. The individual relates ambiguously to himself because he asserts himself by resisting "to become whole."

According to Kierkegaard, this ambiguity characterizes the demonic. He writes that the demonic is anxiety about the good and then that the demonic is determined as "unfreedom that wants to close itself off" (206; 123). But if unfreedom were able to do this, anxiety would not exist. Even if an individual keeps himself in an unfree state, underneath he still maintains a relationship to the good. At the moment that we are affected by the possibility of good, anxiety manifests itself. In anxiety lies not only the resistance to but also the influence by this possibility. That the individual is nonetheless influenced or affected is shown in that he must do something, namely hold on to his resistance. He closes himself up within himself. Kierkegaard writes, "In this lies what is profound about existence, precisely that unfreedom makes itself a prisoner" (207; 124).

This provides us with the central definition of the demonic— and consequently of the anxiety about the good. The demonic is an enclosing reserve, but this must be clarified. An individual can close himself up within himself and then, when the time is ripe, manifest himself. Contrary to this, in the demonic enclosing reserve the individual makes himself unfree. The coherence or continuity in a person's life that is in the concept of the good consists in that the individual acknowledges himself and can therefore manifest himself. In contrast to this, the demonic means an enclosing reserve where the individual closes himself up within himself so that he does not want to reveal himself. This does not exclude that the individual can be outwardly directed, but he is hiding himself by his words and actions. If he expresses himself or manifests himself, it is involuntarily. "Inclosing reserve is precisely muteness. Language, the word, is precisely what saves" (207; 124). I will return to this passage in chapter 7.

The demonic expresses itself in different ways. The starting point is that "there is something that freedom is unwilling to pervade" (213; 130f). Kierkegaard has previously given a couple of examples. In a drunken state a person can do something that he only vaguely remembers; yet he knows that it was so wild that it is almost impossible for him "to recognize himself" (211; 128). Or, a person has once been insane, "and has retained a memory of his former state. …What determines whether the phenomenon is demonic is the individual's attitude toward disclosure, whether he will interpenetrate that fact with freedom and accept it in freedom. Whenever he will not do this, the phenomenon is demonic" (211; 128f). The demonic enclosing reserve is strangely ambiguous, since the individual closes himself up within himself by keeping away what he somewhere has a memory of. By keeping it away he "protects" it; he is precisely relating to what he does not want to interpenetrate in freedom or recognize.

In *The Concept of Anxiety* Kierkegaard attributes a wide range of meaning to the demonic and sees it as being common. The demonic can manifest itself psychosomatically in phenomena such as "a hyper-sensibility and a hyperirritability, neurasthenia, hysteria, hypochondria, etc." (218; 136). But it can also manifests itself "as indolence that postpones thinking, as curiosity that never becomes more than curiosity, as dishonest self-deception, as effeminate weakness that constantly relies on others, as superior negligence, as stupid busyness, etc." (219f; 138). It is, however, important to note that we are dealing with phenomena in which the demonic manifests itself. In other words there must be an enclosing reserve in these phenomena. As an example, a person has reservations when in indolence he postpones thinking or when he does not let his curiosity become anything more than curiosity. I will discuss this further in chapter 4.

The Ambiguity of Anxiety

Even though, in Kierkegaard's words, anxiety lost "its dialectical ambiguity" where the difference between good and evil is concerned, ambiguity returns in anxiety about the good and, moreover, in an intensified form. In Kierkegaard's analysis of anxiety, ambiguity is a key concept that expands as the analysis progresses.

First of all, the situation that produces anxiety is ambiguous or vague insofar as it is undetermined and demands a decision. Furthermore, the possibility that anxiety manifests is itself ambiguous. It is not only the possibility of freedom, it is also the possibility of unfreedom, and this is due to anxiety itself being ambiguous. We relate ambiguously in anxiety when we distance ourselves from what we are anxious about but, at the same time, we are attracted to it. Kierkegaard goes as far as to define anxiety as an ambiguous power. Although anxiety is something we feel ourselves, anxiety also has a power over us. It overwhelms us.

In short, anxiety gives us more than the possibility for discovering ourselves as a self. In anxiety we also relate ambiguously to ourselves. In the demonic enclosing reserve this ambiguity can become two wills, a subordinate and impotent will to reveal ourselves, and one stronger that wills the enclosing reserve (211; 129). In anxiety a person can hide, even from himself.

It is worth noting that the possibility to which anxiety links itself changes through time. Fundamentally, anxiety reveals the possibility of freedom but can also become anxiety of this possibility. In anxiety about evil we relate to the possibility of repeating that which we have realized was evil. In anxiety about the good we struggle against the possibility of "becoming whole." But when anxiety appears, it is because we are affected by the possibility of good against which we struggle. Also in this case anxiety reveals the possibility of freedom although it is hidden.

Kierkegaard's concept of anxiety is complex. By examining the concept of anxiety further it is possible to distinguish two levels in his analysis. On the first level anxiety reveals *the possibility of freedom*. However, this is an ambiguous possibility that makes us feel anxious, and in this anxiety for the possibility of freedom the individual transgresses, and this prefigures the second level. Anxiety is not just the possibility of freedom; in anxiety we also become unfree. On the second level anxiety is more or less distinctly an *unfree self-relation*. This is clearly the case in the anxiety about the good where the individual makes himself unfree by closing himself up within himself.

Among many other things, *The Concept of Anxiety* is an attempt to give the word "anxiety" a pregnant meaning. It is especially Kierkegaard's distinction between fear and anxiety that has left an influence on the way posterity views anxiety. As previously mentioned, fear deals with something specifically, while anxiety has nothing as its object (136; 41). The object of anxiety is "something that is nothing" (137; 43). What does it mean that anxiety has an object but that this object is "nothing"? Anxiety is not without an object. To be sure this object is not something specific, but it is unspecifically something. That is, it points to the situation where things lose their dependability. The situation is characterized by its indefiniteness. In such a situation we are faced with the task of defining ourselves. Anxiety thus points back to ourselves: that we are not automatically ourselves; we have first to become ourselves.

Now the second level of the analysis of anxiety emerges; on this second level anxiety relates to a specific reality. Kierkegaard writes that the object of anxiety is "a determinate something" (196; 111) and its nothingness is really something since the distinction between good and evil is posited (196f; 111f). However, he is not referring to a completely different concept of anxiety. The first level still applies inasmuch as it indicates a requirement that must be fulfilled before anxiety can appear. In order for anxiety to appear, there must be an ambiguous possibility in relation to this specific reality. And it is precisely such an ambiguous possibility that produces the actuality of sin.

The actuality of sin should not continue to exist. That it continues to exist, however, is the possibility that makes us feel anxious because it is continuing by our actions. Thus ambiguity returns where the possibility of salvation is concerned. This possibility is "again a nothing, which the individual both loves and fears (!)" (146; 53).

On a first reading, the two levels that I have distinguished seem to correspond to anxiety "before" the Fall and "after" the Fall. But it is not quite that simple. Kierkegaard compares innocence and anxiety about the good. In innocence the possibility of freedom manifests itself in the individual's anxiety. In anxiety about the good (the demonic) freedom is lost, but "here again freedom's possibility is anxiety" (206; 123). Whereas innocence is a determination leading to freedom, the possibility of freedom is now seen in relation to unfreedom. In a sense the relation is flipped around in the demonic. However, what is essential is that the possibility of freedom also manifests itself in the anxiety about the good. If this were not the case, anxiety would not appear. The relation of the individual to the possibility of good is ambiguous. The individual closes himself within himself to escape this possibility, but he does this precisely because he is affected by it. In addition, the demonic is a state that holds a possibility: it is uncertain what it will become. It depends on the position of the individual. Any further step from a given state is in a sense a "leap" that the individual takes; and in this, the possibility of freedom manifests itself again.

Both levels thus manifest themselves "after" the Fall: freedom is lost in anxiety, but in anxiety the possibility of freedom also reveals itself. This makes it natural to ask if the meaning of anxiety is not itself ambiguous.

The Meaning of Anxiety

What is important to Kierkegaard is to show what anxiety reveals about being a human being. In short, anxiety (meaning that a person can be anxious and referring to the experience that he has in anxiety) reveals that an individual is a self that is not automatically himself, but first has to become himself. In anxiety an individual relates to himself as a spirit or a self. It is natural to raise the objection that if Kierkegaard is right, then anxiety only concerns an individual's relationship to himself, thus isolating the self-relation as a "spiritual" one from the corporality and as an "inwardly" one from the world.

That an individual is a synthesis means that the soul and the body belong together. But everything has not yet been said. For the synthesis will first become a task at the exact moment when the two factors are separated. At that very moment we realize that we are heterogeneous with ourselves; we step out of ourselves. In puberty when we become aware of ourselves we also see ourselves as a body: we become a stranger to ourselves, the body changes and the changes are at the same time ourselves. Even our own voice can change despite the fact that we are so close to it that it is difficult to hear ourselves; for a boy, the voice can suddenly crack so that he can listen to himself and hear a stranger and yet it is himself. Some changes, such as a girl's first period, can create almost a monumental moment.

It is worth noting in Kierkegaard's analysis that even though he does not talk of puberty in any particularly concrete manner, the discovery of ourselves that occurs in anxiety is linked to the experience that follows the body's changes. In order to become a self, the individual first has to experience himself by being distinguished or separated from himself, and this happens fundamentally by corporality changing meaning. As a spirit the individual relates to himself as a body. In

Kierkegaard's words the spirit, meaning man as a self, is determined as body "with a generic difference" (159; 68), as "*genus*" (160; 69). The connection between the factors of the synthesis, which the spirit or the self is supposed to create, is so crucial that a lack of coherence in relation to one factor also manifests itself in relation to the other. As previously quoted, man is "a synthesis of psyche and body sustained by spirit, and therefore a disorganization in one shows itself in the others" (205; 122).

We will not go further into the first part of the objection. The second part of the objection demands that we take a closer look at what is implied in the self-relation. Self-relation means being redoubled, that the individual *himself* relates to something and that through this he relates *to himself* (as someone relating in such and such a way to this and that). When Kierkegaard focuses his attention on the individual's relation to himself, it is important to realize that the self-relation manifests itself in the individual's position towards his surroundings, for example, if in indolence he postpones thinking, if he curiously does not go beyond curiosity or in the absence of self-respect asserts himself. Also in this regard, an individual cannot escape being in a relation to himself. The self-relation is not only implied in the bodily experience of oneself, but also in the way in which the individual bears his past and in the way the individual views his situation. What an individual does, he does with himself.

As I have shown, Kierkegaard attributes a universal meaning to anxiety. As a human possibility (that an individual can be anxious) and as a human experience, anxiety reveals that an individual is a self, determined by the task of becoming himself. But is anxiety an automatic part of human existence? Kierkegaard also understands anxiety "negatively." In anxiety we become unfree since we tie ourselves to an unfree state. If such an anxiety was an automatic part of human life, this anxiety could not be described as unfreedom. On the contrary, the precondition seems to be that human life can only succeed without anxiety. What is essential is to be free of anxiety.

When attributing a universal meaning to anxiety there are problems. Anxiety risks becoming a vague state that spreads out over the whole of human life. This is why it is important to specify what Kierkegaard understands by anxiety. Or rather, to specify that he attributes a variety of meanings to anxiety. When describing the phenomena of anxiety, Kierkegaard is in particular exploring anxiety as an unfree state to which the individual ties himself. But prior to this anxiety there is the anxiety that reveals the possibility of freedom. On this first level anxiety is the possibility of discovering ourselves as a self. This first level is not annulled by the other; on the contrary, we can go from the second level (anxiety as an unfree self-relation) back to the first level (anxiety that reveals the possibility of freedom). For when the unfree state to which we tie ourselves qualifies as anxiety, it is because it is ambiguous. It too is affected by the possibility of freedom. This was shown in an intensified form in the anxiety about the good.

In the beginning of the final chapter (chapter 5), Kierkegaard writes about how every individual must learn to be in anxiety, which is even seen as the ultimate. Thus anxiety is not only that from which a person should free himself, but he also has to learn how to be anxious "in the right way." The anxiety that must be learned is anxiety as the possibility of freedom; "only such anxiety is through faith absolutely educative" (234, 155). The question of the relationship between anxiety and faith, about which the final chapter is concerned, we must postpone until later (chapter 9). But what we have been dealing with so far already implies that freedom does not come without anxiety. For in anxiety the individual discovers freedom as his freedom, as the freedom by which he is defined.

Since the possibility of freedom manifests itself in anxiety, anxiety is thus given a fundamental meaning, This, by far, does not mean that everything has been said since anxiety is also a state of unfreedom. That it is necessary to learn how to be anxious in order to become free of anxiety can be understood in the sense that the way out of the unfreedom to which we tie ourselves goes through anxiety as the possibility of freedom. This creates another question about whether this possibility of freedom does not presuppose the experience of unfreedom. In anxiety an individual also becomes unfree since, in Kierkegaard's words, he "loses himself." Is there a sense in which such a loss of self to become ourselves is necessary? Is it necessary to take the detour that leads us through "the negative"? Also in this sense does an individual have to learn how to be anxious in order to be free—of anxiety?

I will address these questions in the following chapters. In a way I begin all over again in the further examination, namely with the concept of existence. To be sure, Kierkegaard's analysis of anxiety is indirectly an analysis of human existence, but in *The Concept of Anxiety* the word "existence" is used only sporadically with its pregnant meaning. In one passage Kierkegaard writes that the essential is in "the human existence" (124; 28); in another passage he writes of "existential concepts" (227; 147).[9] It is not until *Concluding Unscientific Postscript* that the word "existence" is used recurrently in its pregnant sense; however, Kierkegaard does not make an explicit analysis of anxiety in this

---

[9] Other passages are not as pregnant, including "such an existence" (181; 94), "such a genius-existence" (188; 102), "existence is, as it were, put to a test" (190; 104), and "religious existence" (191; 105).

book.[10] The analysis of existence in *Concluding Unscientific Postscript* actually seems to constitute a new tendency that runs parallel to the analysis of anxiety. The point, however, turns out to be the same: the understanding of man as a self, faced with the task of becoming himself. With good reason, I can put the two analyses together.

---

[10] In reflecting on *The Concept of Anxiety*, Kierkegaard links anxiety with "existence-inwardness" (9, 225; 269) in *Concluding Unscientific Postscript*.

CHAPTER 2

Existence

What a Human Being Is

"But in order to get started, let us state a bold proposition: let us assume that we know what a human being is" (6, 38; 38). This proposal is made by the pseudonymous author Johannes Climacus in *Philosophical Fragments*, published on 13 June 1844, four days before *The Concept of Anxiety*. As was the case with *The Concept of Anxiety*, the name of the pseudonymous author of *Philosophical Fragments* was added. On the title page Kierkegaard's name still appears since *Philosophical Fragments or a Fragment of Philosophy* by Johannes Climacus is "Edited by S. Kierkegaard."

There is a double meaning in Climacus's proposal. The idea is not only that we know what man is. The proposal says we can assume that we know what man is. Thus the proposal implies the question about if, in fact, we do know.

It is one thing to believe we know what man is; it is another thing to propose that we assume we know. What is surprising is not what the assumption says (that we know) but the idea of an assumption we have to make. The point seems to be the contrary: we do not know what man is. In any case we do not know automatically. We must assume that we do. And, moreover, this is daring.

Climacus does not present his daring proposal at the beginning of *Philosophical Fragments*. This does not happen until chapter 3, which begins, as does chapter 1, with Socrates. The first sentence in chapter 1 takes the form of a question: can the truth be learned? Climacus calls this a Socratic question. The

Socratic answer to the question is that "the truth in which I rest was in me and emerged from me" (6, 17; 12). The truth is in the single individual himself. To be sure, an individual begins by having lost or forgotten the truth, but the truth emerges "solely by itself." It may sound a little strange that Climacus speaks about *the* truth without any hesitation, but by using the definite article he means the truth in which the single individual "rests" and on which he can build his life. When the question becomes whether this truth can be communicated, the answer is that an individual cannot give another the truth, but can at the most help the other to find it for herself. For the single individual must find the truth himself, "solely by himself."

However, the character of Socrates in *Philosophical Fragments* has various nuances. The previous description makes it appear that Socrates emphasizes the existential question about truth that the single individual has to appropriate. But that which Climacus has Socrates stand for in chapter 1 of *Philosophical Fragments* is the view that truth can be taken back into eternity so that the historical moment becomes irrelevant. This refers to the teaching of Plato in his *Phaedo*: knowledge is recollection of the world of ideas.

Chapter 3 of *Philosophical Fragments* also starts with a question about truth, but it is now clarified as a question about self-knowledge. The demand is "know thyself!" Socrates himself stands as the best judge of human character. The strange thing is now that this man who knows so much of human character is perplexed about whether he "was a more curious monster than Typhon or a friendlier and simpler being, by nature sharing something divine" (6, 38; 37). When Climacus makes his daring proposal that we assume we know what man is, it is based on Socrates' perplexity; Climacus is arguing this fact with his contemporaries who think they know what man is.

By contrast, Climacus's proposal can be understood in this way: that we have ignorance as a starting point, and consequently have to begin by acknowledging it. That we must assume—in order to get started at all—that we know what man is, seems to point back to the fact that we really do not know. To acknowledge this ignorance gives us another starting point. It is in this admitted ignorance that we can pose the question about what man is. It even seems to be crucial to pose the question in this way in order to preserve humanity.

Man Is Indeed Existing

Johannes Climacus goes on to write a second book, namely *Concluding Unscientific Postscript to Philosophical Fragments*, which was published in February of 1846—again "Edited by S. Kierkegaard." Kierkegaard had intended this book to be the end of his authorship.[1] *Concluding Unscientific Postscript* (which is 500 to 600 pages) is a postscript to *Philosophical Fragments* (which is about 100 pages). The question about what man is repeated in *Concluding Unscientific Postscript*; but Climacus seems to be in a hurry to answer it, and the answer even seems to be repeated monotonously: man is existing.

In *Concluding Unscientific Postscript* Climacus is in constant polemic against the effort to perceive existence (*tilværelsen*) as a system, that is to say, as a closed whole. It is possible that existence (*tilværelsen*) is a system to God, but an individual's attempt to grasp it speculatively as a system is comic, for what is a human being? As a human being "he is indeed existing" (9, 103; 120), and as existing he is in process, or as Climacus states it, "in the process of becoming."

---

[1] *Concluding Unscientific Postscript, Supplement*, vol. II, p. 167 (Pap. X 6 B 249 s. 410).

When Climacus states that man is indeed existing, it seems as if he is reminding us of something that is obvious. Automatically every individual is existing, and yet the concept of existence is stressed. We can apparently exist in different ways, so that what is important is really to exist.

Thus there must be something that intervenes to complicate the obvious, i.e., that man is existing, and this is the fact that it is possible to forget that we exist. Following up on the sentence that man is indeed existing (the individual who was to think out the system), Climacus states,

> Now, all in all, there are two ways for an existing individual: either he can do everything to forget that he is existing and thereby manage to become comic (the comic contradiction of wanting to be what one is not, for example, that a human being wants to be a bird is no more comic than the contradiction of not wanting to be what one is, as *in casu* (in this case) an existing individual, just as in the use of language it is comic when someone forgets his name, which signifies not so much forgetting his name as the singularity of his nature), because existence possesses the remarkable quality that an existing person exists whether he wants to or not; or he can direct all his attention to his existing. (9, 103; 120)

Even though we exist, regardless of whether we want to or not, it seems crucial that we remember it. Climacus directs his passionate polemic against this forgetfulness of being someone who exists. It is worth noting that it is not just some philosophers lost in thought who forget this. If this forgetfulness does not distinguish Kierkegaard's time, at least it characterizes it. Climacus's critical formula, which he returns to time and time again, reads like this: time has forgotten what it means to exist. "My main thought was that, because of the copiousness of knowledge, people in our day have forgotten what it means *to exist*, and what *inwardness* is" (9, 208; 249).

The Difficulty of Existence

To the question of what a human being is, Climacus apparently answers by saying that a human being is existing. But the question is repeated: what does it mean to exist? What is implied in this question is what it means to exist as a human being. Or again, what is it to be a human being? Climacus emphasizes that the question is not what it means to be a human being in general, "but what it means that we, you and I and he, are human beings, each one on his own" (9, 103; 120).

When Climacus' diagnosis states that time has forgotten what it means to exist, we might be tempted to think there must be a specific answer to the question. If the problem is that time has forgotten what it means to exist, then it must be possible to say what it means to exist as a human being. That which time has forgotten certainly has to be something specific. The *Concluding Unscientific Postscript*, however, offers no specific answer. Climacus's insistent repetition of time having forgotten what it means to exist seems almost to step in as a substitute for an answer.

We must also ask what an answer should consist of. If the point is that "you and I and he, are human beings, each one on his own," it seems that we can only give an individual answer to the question.

However, the forgetfulness not only consists in that we have forgotten what it means to be a human being. We have forgotten it "because of the copiousness of knowledge" as it was stated in a previous passage. But in order to forget what it means to exist, it is not sufficient that we know a lot of other things; we also have to make ourselves important with this other knowledge, and attribute a meaning to this knowledge in a way that it is not necessary to pose the question about what it means to exist. The point is not just that knowledge of what it means to be a human being is repressed by another knowledge or the accumulation of knowledge. The forgetfulness of what it means to be a human being occurs since we think we know. We do not need to make the daring assumption that we know. We think we know, and thus we do not pose the question about what it means to exist. The forgetfulness consists in that we forget to ask. The forgetfulness that is dangerous is to believe that we know what it means to be a human being, so that we do not need to pose the question, and, consequently, the question itself loses its meaning.

Climacus describes the problem both in speculative thought and in Kierkegaard's time this way: we ignore the difficulty of existence, that is to say the problem in existing. Normally a problem is something we should solve or that should be cleared up for us so that we can carry on with our lives. The problem we are dealing with here, however, does not go away, and it is not supposed to. On the contrary, we only understand what it means to exist if we understand the problem involved. Thus the problem consists in the *task* that existing puts before the existing individual. Fundamentally, the problem is what we do with our lives.

When the question is what it means to exist, there is therefore already an answer in recognizing that there is a problem or a task in existing. As a counter-move to forgetfulness, Climacus can thus insist on the difficulty or the problem instead of giving the answer a specific content.

So far it seems as if we end up with the answer that we are human beings, each one on his own. We need—individually—to find an answer to the question or the problem of existing, and we do this by the way we individually understand our lives.

However, the problem does have a shared characteristic. The previous discussion has already hinted at what existence means. There are two fundamental features: first, as existing, we are in process, in the process of becoming; second, we are placed in relation to ourselves since we are confronted with the problem of existing. These two fundamental features (to be in the process of becoming and to be in a self-relation) come together as the task of becoming ourselves.

The further determination of the concept or the problem of existence thus leads us to the same insight as was found in the analysis of anxiety: an individual is a self-relation in the fundamental sense that he is faced with the task of becoming himself. But different from the analysis of anxiety, we have here started with the question about what man is and with an ignorance that leaves room for the question. And in a certain sense we have not put the question behind us inasmuch as the question turns out to be a part of being a human being. The answer to what it means to exist is only found by our understanding the problem or the difficulty implied in existing.

Subjectivity and (Un)Truth

In *Philosophical Fragments* Climacus begins by posing the question of whether the truth can be learned. Without further ado he talks about *the* truth, and we could get the impression that there is a common truth from the start. What was otherwise said about the truth seemed, however, to give the opposite impression, for the individual has the truth within himself. The truth can only be "learned" or communicated by the single individual finding it.

The single individual knows within himself what it means to exist.

In *Concluding Unscientific Postscript* Climacus expresses it this way: "Subjectivity is truth" (9, 169; 203). This sounds as if each individual himself decides what is true, i.e., as if the single individual himself is the yardstick, but also here this first impression does not correspond to reality. Climacus makes a little addition: "Subjectivity, inwardness is truth" (9, 170; 204). Instead of subjectivity automatically deciding what is the truth, subjectivity itself is defined. The subjectivity that is the truth is inwardness, appropriation, or passion. Thus the question is more about the way we relate to what is to be considered as the truth. We can only speak about truth when the truth becomes the truth for us as single individuals. It is only true when it is true for me. That is to say that the single individual changes in this relation. The truth under discussion is, as mentioned, the truth in which we "rest" and that which we are thus determined in relation to. To decide for this truth is to be determined.

This is emphasized not only by Climacus's little addition, but he also adds another sentence: "Subjectivity, inwardness, is truth. Is there *a more inward* expression for it? Yes, if the discussion about 'Subjectivity, inwardness, is truth' begins in this way: 'Subjectivity is untruth'" (9, 173; 207). We now have two sentences: "Subjectivity is truth" and "Subjectivity is untruth." The second sentence seems to contradict the first. But not only does the second not cancel the first; the second sentence is the way in which the first is to begin. That is to say that with the second sentence we take a step backwards to another beginning. This gives us a more inward expression of the previous statement that subjectivity, inwardness, is the truth. What does this mean?

The second sentence has its origin in *Philosophical Fragments*. As mentioned, Climacus begins by outlining what he calls the Socratic question and the Socratic answer. But this creates a springboard from which he can develop an alternative to the Socratic, namely the thought that the single individual is "untruth" and is so "solely by himself." Climacus then suggests that we call this state of being "untruth" due to our own fault "sin" (6, 20; 15).

Consequently, we have another beginning different from that of the Socratic. By turning inward, the individual does not discover that he already holds the truth; instead he discovers his own untruth. Climacus adds that in a certain sense the Socratic still applies here, "because I can discover my own untruth only by myself, because only when *I* discover it is it discovered, not before, even though the whole world knew it" (6, 19; 14).

The *Concluding Unscientific Postscript* seeks to elucidate this rather complex connection by having the two sentences stand in opposition to each other: "Subjectivity is truth" and "Subjectivity is untruth." That subjectivity is the untruth is another beginning in relation to the Socratic. Climacus writes, "But now existence has accentuated the existing person a second time; a change so essential has taken place in him that he in no way can take himself back into eternity by Socratically recollecting" (9, 173; 207-08).[2] The first time an individual is "accentuated" or marked, it is by being situated in relation to the eternal truth that the existing individual must appropriate. When we are marked by something, we become somebody else than we were before the change. This is also what happens when the individual is marked a second time, but here the change is "essential" since he is not marked by something else; he is marked by himself. He is

---

[2] Howard and Edna Hong translate *mærket* into "accentuated"; I use "marked" in the sense "left its mark on." Trans.

marked or defined by being in untruth and this by his own doing. However, this requires that he must realize untruth and appropriate it, and in this way the first sentence is repeated (the demand that one discover the truth about oneself: one's own untruth). Self-consciousness is altered in that we become another, and we can no longer recognize ourselves. We are turned inward but in a way that we have a beginning outside ourselves. Thus Climacus can maintain "that subjectivity, inwardness, is truth, is my thesis" (9, 235; 278).

Thus again the key concepts are inwardness and appropriation. It is particularly the concept of inwardness that is difficult to come to terms with. It is natural to associate inwardness with an inner space or an inner life. In Kierkegaard's works he at times writes about inwardness that can be so inward that it does not have an expression. But inwardness is especially linked to an act, though it is a particular act. Climacus talks about the act in the eminent sense of the word, that is to say "not in terms of achievement but in terms of inwardness" (10, 12; 304). We can interpret this to mean what an individual does with himself when he acts. When he does something outwardly, maybe even an achievement, the act also has an effect on him. Thus inwardness is also connected to understanding. "The inwardness of the understanding" means that the single individual understands the truth solely by himself (9, 67; 77). Inwardness contains an understanding of ourselves, namely that which an individual understands by what he does. Or, rather, there is the requirement to understand what we do. Hence, inwardness is something that can be absent. That inwardness is absent manifests itself by our not taking responsibility for what we do. We do not allow it to go inward.

Thus the inwardness contains the requirement of appropriation, but inwardness also means that the single individual, by virtue of being placed before himself, already stands apart from other people and can therefore turn against his surroundings. In other words, inwardness is linked to being a human being. This is significant for the understanding of the relationship between people. This is a relationship that is broken or reflected in the single individual in the sense that in order to be a true relation, the single individual's self-activity (*selvvirksomhed*) is required. Since inwardness means that the single individual also deals with himself in relation to others and thus can answer for his actions towards others, Climacus can state that "the ethical is inwardness" (9, 118; 143) and that "inwardness is the individual's relation to himself before God" (10, 124; 436-37).

Thus subjectivity is further determined as inwardness, but Climacus also uses the concepts of appropriation and passion— almost indiscriminately. How do these determinations of subject- tivity relate to each other? As shown, the requirement implied in inwardness is a requirement for appropriation. Climacus can therefore talk about "the appropriation of inwardness." What about passion then? On a first reading, passion seems to move in the opposite direction of inwardness. Passion is the movement that goes "beyond" ourselves, whereas inwardness goes inward, but in passion there is, nevertheless, a movement that returns to us. Passion is concerned with what is "other" to us, that which we are determined in relation to. This is manifest in the beginning of chapter 3 of *Philosophical Fragments* to which I just referred. Here it is stated that the passion of thought is to think what cannot be thought, and that the passion of love deals with the other person rather than with us. But at the same time passion is completed in this movement that goes "beyond" us. It may sound strange to speak of completion since in passion we reach a limitation for ourselves, but through this limitation we can also come to ourselves.

In other words, passion is a determination of subjectivity because it consists of a self-relation. Passion means that we engage in something, that there is an important difference that something matters. However, passion takes on different forms. There is more; it can go in circles so that we imprison ourselves. The movement then becomes self-encircling.

This brings us back to *The Concept of Anxiety*. It is true that Kierkegaard in his analysis of anxiety does not talk as much about (un)truth as about (un)freedom, but he does link the two themes. The enclosing reserve "signifies a lie or, if one prefers, untruth. But untruth is precisely unfreedom which is anxious about disclosure" (210 fn; 128 fn). This gives us an opportunity to understand further what in an abstract way Climacus calls untruth both in *Philosophical Fragments* and in *Concluding Unscientific Postscript*. To be in untruth is to be unfree since we make ourselves unfree. *The Concept of Anxiety* also indicates that we can depart from unfreedom via the truth. Again Kierkegaard speaks about the truth using the definite article. The truth does something to the individual; in fact it does something essential since it "makes man free" (220; 138). At the same time, Kierkegaard emphasizes the requirement for appropriation since "truth is for the particular individual only as he himself produces it in action" (220; 138). As in the biblical book of John, we are dealing with the truth that frees the individual (John 8:32) and that the individual must do the truth (John 3:21).

Kierkegaard does not use the word "appropriation" here. Instead, inwardness becomes a key concept since it becomes the positive counterpart in the further analysis of the demonic or the anxiety for the good. Inwardness is that the truth to the single individual is construed in such a way that he himself brings it about by acting. If the single individual prevents the truth in being this way to himself, we have "a phenomenon of the demonic" (220; 138), and such a phenomenon is characterized by the absence of inwardness.

Again inwardness is linked to action as well as understanding. "Certitude and inwardness, which can be attained only by and in action, determine whether or not the individual is demonic" (220; 138-39). Further on in the book we read that "inwardness is an understanding" (223; 142), but in such a way that we understand ourselves in that which we say (223; 142). Inwardness in this sense is earnestness (226; 146), which again stands for personality itself (229; 149).

Anxiety for the good, the demonic, is not just unfreedom; it is a way to lose freedom. Kierkegaard is describing what he calls "negative phenomena" (220; 139), which, as phenomena of the demonic, are characterized by anxiety. We are dealing with unbelief-superstition, hypocrisy-offense and cowardice-pride. When Kierkegaard links these opposite phenomena, it is because individually they lack the same thing: inwardness.

The difference in passion that we have arrived at turns out indirectly to have a decisive meaning in *The Concept of Anxiety*. Anxiety for the good, the demonic, is further determined as enclosing reserve which is in direct opposition to inwardness. Passion in inwardness is to understand ourselves in relation to the other human being, so that we understand ourselves in that which we say to the other and thus when we try to understand the other. Contrary to this, the passion of enclosing reserve revolves around itself. This is the difference between freedom and unfreedom.

CHAPTER 3

Freedom—and Unfreedom

Anxiety and Choice

Both the interpretation of anxiety (chapter 1 above) and the further determination of the concept or the problem of existence (chapter 2) lead to the understanding that a human being is a self who is faced with the task of becoming himself. Kierkegaard articulates this understanding by means of the concept of freedom.

As mentioned in chapter 1, there is a connection between anxiety and freedom. The connection is so decisive that *The Concept of Anxiety* can be seen as a monograph about freedom. Characteristically enough, Kierkegaard writes about *the* anxiety and *the* freedom, and especially when the two are linked together. Or, as Kierkegaard put it, anxiety is the possibility of freedom. But despite his use of the definite article, anxiety was shown to be ambiguous. Maybe this also applies to freedom; in any case, it can be difficult to determine what Kierkegaard understands by freedom. He speaks of "true, positive freedom." This passage (from *Either/Or*, 3, 163; 173f) is not accidental. On the contrary, it seems to indicate that what Kierkegaard seeks to pinpoint what in different contexts equals true freedom. But if we can discern such a true freedom, then in relation to what is it true? Is that which we otherwise call freedom an illusion? Or is there a freedom that is real enough but different from "true" freedom?

It is reasonable to begin by looking at what Kierkegaard understands by choice. Even though the concept of choice is not explicitly a key term in *The Concept of Anxiety*, it seems implicitly to be so. The analysis of anxiety revealed that anxiety is the possibility of freedom, but we answer this possibility through the choice we make. If we are in a situation with different possibilities, we say that we have different possibilities of choices. Maybe we can also wait and see if other possibilities arise that are better than the ones with which we are presented. Now, the possibility of freedom, as anxiety so precisely revealed, is not a possibility among other possibilities. As we saw earlier, the possibility of freedom that "announces itself" in anxiety is peculiarly persistent. While freedom ordinarily seems to consist in having possibilities that we can choose between, here we are dealing with one possibility, the possibility of freedom. We take up this possibility by choosing. It shows simultaneously that we can and that we must choose. The possibility of freedom manifested in anxiety thus demands that we choose or define ourselves. It is a persistent possibility because we cannot escape the choice. In this sense it is the choice or the necessity of choosing that manifests itself in anxiety, that is, in the possibility of freedom."

When Kierkegaard states that anxiety is or reveals the possibility of freedom, we can ask if in fact it is not the possibility of freedom that *produces* anxiety. At first we would say that what produces anxiety is what we are anxious about. But if anxiety does not concern anything specific, then what produces anxiety? The answer seems to be that it is the possibility of freedom as our own possibility. That which produces anxiety is the fact that the situation we are in depends on ourselves, and that we therefore have to make a choice.

In this way the analysis of anxiety refers back to the concept of choice. Then what does Kierkegaard understand by choice? The concept of choice is first and foremost examined in

Either/Or (published February 1843), or rather in the second half of the work, which, as the title page indicates, contains "Contains the Papers of B, Letters to A," while the first half of the work includes "Contains A's Papers."

Choice of Choice or "Choosing the Choice"

Not only does B, Judge Wilhelm, write to A, but he also writes about A. He goes so far as to want to tell what A is: as an aesthete, A is in despair. B does this by putting two "life-views" up against each other, the aesthetic and the ethical. B places himself in the latter. He writes about his "category," namely choosing (3, 198; 213) his "Either/Or."

However, A also has an "Either/Or." In the first half of the book, we even find "an aesthetic discourse" with the heading "Either/Or." This magnificent piece begins this way:

> Marry, and you will regret it. Do not marry, and you will also regret it. Marry or do not marry, you will regret it either way. Whether you marry or you do not marry, you will regret it either way. Laugh at the stupidities of the world, and you will regret it; weep over them, and you will also regret it. Laugh at the stupidities of the world or weep over them, you will regret it either way. Whether you laugh at the stupidities of the world or you weep over them, you will regret it either way. Trust a girl, and you will regret it. Do not trust her, and you will also regret it. Trust a girl or do not trust her, you will regret it either way. Whether you trust a girl or do not trust her, you will regret it either way. Hang yourself, and you will regret it. Do not hang yourself, and you will also regret it. Hang yourself or do not hang yourself, you will regret it

either way. Whether you hang yourself or do not hang
yourself, you will regret it either way. This, gentlemen,
is the quintessence of all the wisdom of life. (2, 40; 38f)

It is clear why B needs to tell A that his either/or is
completely different from A's. B actually says that A does not
have any concept of what it means to choose. He calls on A to
make a choice: "either-or" (3, 149; 157). Responding to A's
wisdom of life, he says that "your view of life is concentrated in
one single sentence: 'I say simply Either-Or'" (3, 151; 159).
When A simply says either-or he denies the meaning of choice;
when he talks about choice he prevents choice. A's choice is "an
esthetic choice, but an esthetic choice is no choice" (3, 157; 166).

When B speaks about choice, he attributes a certain
meaning to it. At first a strange thing happens: we are taken one
step back from the concrete choice we may be in. For *the*
choice—using the definite article—is not so much the individual,
specific choice we may or may not make. The way that B speaks
about choice reveals that the point is to become aware of the
choice or the meaning of choice. The choice in this context
means to choose; hence it seems to be detached from its meaning
with respect to content (as the choice of one thing or another).
This resembles features that we encountered in the analysis of
anxiety. The movement we get a glimpse of puts us at a distance
to the concrete choice-situation (in which we can otherwise be
absorbed) so that we are faced with the fact that we must choose.

When B emphasizes the choice, a redoubling happens. The
choice he refers to is not so much a choice of one thing or
another but a choice of the choice. This may sound a little far-
fetched, but the idea makes good sense. While the aesthete A
actually does not choose, choosing "is an intrinsic and stringent
term for the ethical" (3, 157; 166). For "the only absolute

Either/Or is the choice between good and evil" (3, 157; 166-67). This is so because choosing the good excludes choosing evil. While the individual in other choices can try to unite the two possibilities, the choice here is an alternative: either good or evil.

Now, B specifies what he means by *the* choice. "Rather than designating the choice between good and evil, my Either-Or designates the choice by which one chooses good and evil or rules them out" (3, 159; 169). According to B, the aesthete denies meaning of choice. The aesthetical is therefore not evil *per se* but "the indifferent." The contrast to the indifferent is "choosing to will" (ibid.). In other words, the first, fundamental choice is to give a critical significance to choice—and in this sense it is a choice of the choice. But the choice that must be made and therefore be given an essential meaning is the choice between good and evil.

B apparently speaks about two choices: the first choice is about choosing to will, and the second choice is about choosing between good and evil. Thus he writes, "What takes precedence in my Either/Or is, then, the ethical. Therefore, the point is not the reality of that which is chosen but the reality of choosing" (3, 166; 176). This is the redoubling I touched on earlier. The choice with content ("the reality of that which is chosen") stands aside in order to allow the meaning of choosing ("the reality of choosing") to step forward. However, B later makes a retreat. There is in fact only one single choice. For the choice to which we must attribute meaning is, after all, a specific choice, namely the absolute choice between good and evil. With the first choice (of the choice between good and evil), the second (between good and evil) is posited. But once again, B specifies that there is only one single choice, and "through this choice, I actually do not choose between good and evil, but I choose the good, but when I choose the good, I choose *eo ipso* the choice between good and evil" (3, 203; 219). The first, fundamental choice is a choice that attributes critical meaning to the difference between good and evil, but this choice we make by choosing the good.

B gets into the apparent redoubling (the choice of the choice, choosing to will) because in A he believes that he is faced with the indifferent where the difference that determines the ethical has lost its meaning. Therefore what matters is choosing the ethical point of view. But how do we choose this if not by choosing the good?

So B uses the aesthete to make the meaning of the ethical stand out. The idea is to choose between living aesthetically or ethically. "But what does it mean to live aesthetically, and what does it mean to live ethically?" (3, 167; 178), B asks himself. We have received a preliminary answer to the latter, but what does "aesthetically" mean?

The Aesthetical—and the Ethical

B answers his own question: "the esthetic in a person is that by which he spontaneously and immediately is what he is; the ethical is that by which he becomes what he becomes" (3, 167; 178). This may not make us any wiser, for B's answer demands an explanation. As a start, let us stick with the expression "immediate." A person is what he is immediately before he takes a position on it.

This is, however, only a first meaning of the aesthetical. According to B, the aesthetical is also a life-view. If we still stay with this first meaning, this life-view must stick to the immediate in the sense of that which is in the moment, or rather what we seek in the moment. An individual can set different goals for himself, but if his search is determined by the moment, the moment itself is determined by what he can get out of it. And this is a satisfaction or pleasure defined by the sensuous (the aesthetical goes back to the Greek word for sensation). But we must not understand this too narrowly. To seek fame, honor and wealth is also to let ourselves be absorbed in the moment.

However, the aesthetical is not yet exhausted. The aesthetical is highly complex, if not ambiguous. B describes different "stages" (as he himself says) within the aesthetical life-view. The last aesthetical stage is where A is to be found, because so far A does not fit the description very well. A is not immediate but reflective. He is not immediately absorbed in the moment; on the contrary, he sees through the emptiness in this search to fill out the moment. Either-Or means to him that no matter what you choose, you will regret it.

B summarizes the different stages within the aesthetical life-view as something that looks like a diagnosis: "every esthetic view of life is despair," "everyone who lives esthetically is in despair, whether he knows it or not" (3, 180; 192). Despair is to let our life be absorbed by what is determined by the moment, in what is now, but may not be in the next moment. For a human being is obliged to be beyond the moment with a memory of the past and questioning the future. As mentioned, there is a last stage within the aesthetical (A, for an example) and "this last life-view is despair itself" (3, 181; 194). A is linked to immediacy inasmuch as he seeks diversion in the moment, but at the same time he sees the emptiness in this search, and in this sense he is outside himself, namely in despair. A's special position within the aesthetical life-view is that he is, to a certain degree, conscious of "the nothingness of such a life-view" (ibid.). In a sense, B actually needs A to describe the aesthetical life-view as despair.

B also needs A in order to articulate what the ethical consists of. This is not only in the sense that the ethical achieves its meaning in opposition to the aesthetical. B must explicitly or implicitly refer to the experience of a threatening nothingness that A expresses. A previous stage within the aesthetical is the life-view that "health is the most precious good, is that around which everything revolves." B observes that the same view is given a more poetic expression in the statement, "Beauty is the ultimate" (3, 170; 181). In both cases we can let our life be summarized in being healthy and beautiful, or maybe particularly in being viewed as healthy and beautiful by others. However, we are more than that, and this can manifest itself when we may no longer be healthy or beautiful, or when we are not viewed as healthy and beautiful by others. That which B wants to express is exactly this consciousness of being more than what we are immediately determined to be: i.e., healthy, beautiful, and rich—or maybe precisely the opposite, sick, ugly, and poor. An aesthetical life-view can consist of comforting ourselves with the knowledge that we are (considered to be) a success so that we do not see ourselves as being in despair. In a certain sense, A falls outside the aesthetical, for when he realizes the emptiness or the nothingness that threatens him, he sees through this knowledge that at first glance seems secure.

Even though A is in despair, he does not really despair. To be sure, we can speak of his sense of nothingness, but it is not the dizziness of anxiety where we lose our footing. On the contrary, A keeps himself in a noncommittal (*svævende*) state. Despair is therefore not permitted to break through. B writes to A, "you continually hover [*svæve*] above yourself" (3, 185; 198). A's despair does not force him back on himself.

This is exactly what happens in anxiety. What anxiety is supposed to reveal is that the individual himself is more than what he is determined or viewed to be. Anxiety detaches the individual from the context by which he would otherwise be absorbed. This consciousness of being something other and more than what we are determined to be is the consciousness of being a person. This means that we act and see for ourselves; we are not just viewed as doing so. Thus, "person" becomes a key concept in B's determination of the ethical.

What then is the ethical? B writes to A, "You know how to calculate the moment; you are sentimental, heartless, all according to the circumstances; but during all this you are at all times only in the moment, and for that reason your life disintegrates, and it is impossible for you to explain it" (3, 168; 179). B writes that what A lacks is "memory of your own life" (3, 184; 197). Contrary to this, the ethical is to strive for coherence or to gain continuity in our life, and consequently to help us to become aware of ourselves. Without this striving for coherence, our life could otherwise be dispersed at one or another moment. Again B formulates this as a choice: to choose ourselves in our eternal validity. It is to become free. We can even say that an individual only becomes free through the choice.

Choice and Freedom

When choice is given such an important meaning in Kierkegaard's writings, it is precisely because freedom does not seem to exist without a choice. That an individual can and must choose is an expression of his freedom, and the individual only becomes free in an accentuated sense by choosing.

At the same time, what is strange is that Kierkegaard now seems to deny that the individual has the freedom to choose. Both in *Either/Or* and in *The Concept of Anxiety*, he rejects the notion of a *liberum arbitrium*, which means free choice or free decision in Latin.

Thus we read in *Either/Or*, "I am by no means confusing *liberum arbitrium* with true, positive freedom" (3, 163; 173-74). This leaves the reader with a question about what it is that B does not confuse. He does not say much about this himself, either about *liberum arbitrium* or the true positive freedom, but the point seems to be this: *liberum arbitrium* means the ability to choose the good as well as the evil. When we choose, we choose "either" one thing "or" the other without making the alternative essential. In the same way, we could have chosen something other than what we chose. The ability or freedom to choose is not determined by what is chosen. Thus, *liberum arbitrium* is an unspecific freedom. True freedom is, however, determined by the fact that it has evil outside of it as "a weak possibility," as B states it. Freedom becomes true freedom by excluding the possibility of evil. It is not the freedom to choose but *freedom* that becomes manifest by a choice, namely by choosing the good.

This is only to say that *liberum arbitrium* is not the true positive freedom. However, *The Concept of Anxiety* makes it clear that the thought of *liberum arbitrium* itself is rejected. And that is all it is, a thought, an abstraction, not even a thought-thing but a "nuisance for thought." The thought is explicitly rejected in two places in *The Concept of Anxiety*; let us take a closer look at these rejections. The first reads, "Nor can there be any anxiety if sin came into the world by an act of an abstract *liberum arbitrium* (which no more existed in the world in the beginning than in a late period, because it is a nuisance for thought)" (143; 49). And the second reads, "To maintain that freedom begins as *liberum arbitrium* (which is found nowhere, cf. Leibniz) that can choose good just as well as evil inevitably makes every explanation impossible" (197; 112).

As we can see, the two passages run parallel to each other. In both passages the rejection of the notion is put in brackets.

Liberum arbitrium is a "nuisance for thought," i.e., something "which is found nowhere." But what does *liberum arbitrium* mean when it can be rejected as a nuisance for thought? As for this question, the second passage tells us a little more than the first. *Liberum arbitrium* can "choose good just as well as evil."

The passage is taken from the beginning of chapter 4 of *The Concept of Anxiety*. As we saw earlier, the idea is that "the object of anxiety is a determinate something and its nothing is an actual something, because the distinction between good and evil is posited *in concreto*" (196f; 111f). The meaning of the latter part of the passage is explained in a long note where freedom is linked to the difference between good and evil. If we understand the difference between good and evil in an abstract manner, we make freedom into something other than what it is, namely, "an object of thought." The note then explains, "But freedom is never *in abstracto*. If freedom is given a moment to choose between good and evil, a moment when freedom itself is in neither the one nor the other, then in that very moment freedom is not freedom, but a meaningless reflection" (196; 111f., fn). To understand the difference between good and evil as an abstract difference means that we have the difference outside of ourselves. But this is precisely what we have in the unspecific freedom to choose.

Thus what Kierkegaard rejects is the notion of freedom as the ability to choose good and evil indifferently, that is to say, to choose between good and evil *without* being in one or the other. If we can indifferently choose between good and evil, we are situated outside of both possibilities: we are faced with both possibilities and can freely, arbitrarily, throw our weight onto one or the other side of the scale.

As we saw earlier, B speaks in *Either/Or* about the critical choice between good and evil, and in the note I just quoted it also states that the difference between good and evil first is "for" freedom and "in" freedom. Thus Kierkegaard does not deny that the individual is in a situation where he must choose between good and evil; on the contrary, it is this difference on which it all depends. But in this choice there is in fact only one thing to choose—the good. We do not choose between different possibilities that we are faced with. The freedom that Kierkegaard speaks about is already determined in relation to the good. In the note from *The Concept of Anxiety*, it even states that the good is freedom.

When the difference between good and evil is so critical, it means that we are determined in relation to it in two different ways. First, faced with the choice, we are not at a zero point. We already have a personal history that has marked us; we have already begun in the sense that we have previously made choices and failed. Consequently, we have a history that is heavy with guilt. Second, we are already determined in relation to the possibility of good. This is, as previously mentioned, not a possibility among other possibilities; on the contrary, it is the possibility of becoming ourselves and therefore of becoming free. When the note states that the good is freedom, we must understand it this way: the good is that by which we become free.

True Freedom

Kierkegaard's reflections on coining the concept of choice, along with similar reflections on coining the concept of existence, have probably been the most influential part of his philosophy. In both cases he has taken a concept that we use in our daily life and accentuated its meaning. But when Kierkegaard stresses or distinguishes choice in this manner, it is natural to understand that the choosing is the point more than what we choose. As mentioned, Kierkegaard speaks about the choice of the choice. Within this context, choice has often been understood as a subjective choice in the sense that it is solely the single individual who decides what he will choose. It all depends on the choice.

However, it has been shown to us that when we speak about *the* choice we speak about a specific choice. And the human being who will make a choice is not solely independent in this choice; the individual is not only the one who determines, but he is also determined in the choice. We will go further into this point. We have already seen that in the choice as a choice between good and evil the single individual is determined in relation to the critical difference between good and evil. First, we already have a past to carry around; second, we are determined by the possibility of the good. As we shall see, this becomes one since the fundamental choice is about choosing ourselves.

This is the conclusion that the ethicist B reaches in *Either/Or*. B proclaimed that every aesthetical life-view is despair whether the individual knows it or not. What is unique about A is that he is in despair and knows it. Nevertheless, he does not allow despair to penetrate. That is why B's encouraging advice to A is "despair!" It may sound a little strange to give this advice to a human being whom one claims is in despair, but B's opinion is that A does not take despair seriously and therefore does not take himself seriously. When B says "despair!" he encourages A to choose despair, and choosing despair does not so much mean throwing ourselves into it or seeking it but taking responsibility for the despair that we are already in.

B also expresses this with a different term that appears in *The Concept of Anxiety*, but B gives it a characteristic spin. The encouragement or maybe the requirement ends up sounding like this: we must repent. It is not only A who has to do this but every single individual. And he is not only to repent one thing or another that he has done wrong; he must "repent himself" and even repent the past he comes from, the history of his race (3, 201; 216). This seems to be such an unreasonable demand that we have to ask what the point is. What does it mean to repent in this case? It is to bring our life back in the sense that we appropriate it. The life that is already one's own should be made to one's own, for even if it is already our own life, we can be unclear about it.

Consequently we have been given a condition of what it means to choose ourselves. According to B we can only choose ourselves by repenting ourselves; it is not until we have "repented" ourselves that we are "concrete" (3, 229; 248). On a first reading this looks strange, but repenting ourselves, to use B's expression, is to obtain ourselves, that is, we get ourselves back. This presupposes that in one sense or another we are lost to ourselves. The aesthetical life-view and the aesthetical way of living one's life is lost in the immediate moment—we live in dispersion. The ethical, therefore, becomes the requirement to pull ourselves together, to become clear about ourselves. Thus, to choose ourselves means becoming ourselves in the sense of coming to ourselves.

To choose ourselves is not to create ourselves. B says explicitly, "but I do not create myself—I choose myself" (3, 200; 215). Previously he specified it in this way: "The *I* chooses itself or, more correctly, receives itself" (3, 166; 177). To choose ourselves in the sense that we come back to ourselves is to receive ourselves.

But to receive ourselves is also something we do or must do. Of course *the* choice is a specific choice since we are to choose ourselves, which means becoming that which we already are, but, at the same time, the choice creates a crucial difference. This difference consists in obtaining coherence in the life that is already our own, and therefore to become aware of ourselves. Thus the difference is the appropriation that the choice gives. However, an accent is added when B speaks about "receiving" ourselves. We must do something specific, namely acknowledge ourselves; the individual "acknowledges identity with himself" (3, 200; 216), and this indicates that the problem lies in accepting ourselves.

As we already touched on in chapter 1, a human being is determined as spirit. This means that he must become aware of himself, obtain self-consciousness, or, as B puts it, spirit wants the individual "consciously to possess himself" (3, 175; 186). In a sense B can also say that the individual only comes into existence by choosing himself. He pinpoints a "dialectic" of choice: choice brings about a decisive difference in the sense that what the individual will choose only comes into existence in the choice, but, at the same time, what I choose must already be "posited." What I must choose is myself. He who must choose is an already determined self. He must choose himself as this specific self; in other words, we must "take over" ourselves. Thus to choose ourselves is to become this specific individual that we already are. But, as mentioned, this implies that we were "lost" to ourselves. To choose ourselves is to win back ourselves or to gain determination, since we get a coherence or identity with ourselves.

This is what Kierkegaard means by "true" freedom. Freedom is to be free, but first we have to become free, and we become free by becoming ourselves. Here freedom means being in accordance with oneself or self-agreement. Self-agreement does not mean that in a completely independent manner we can choose what we define as good. Freedom means self-determination that almost becomes the opposite of subjective arbitrariness. Each individual must define himself, and this must be understood in a double sense: he must define himself in the direct sense that he decides or determines himself, but he must decide in such a way that he "gathers himself together." In this way what the individual determines is himself. The individual must determine himself in a more indirect sense so that he determines who he is. As mentioned, that which the individual must determine himself as is this specific individual that he already is. Freedom does not consist in recreating ourselves, but in finding ourselves.

In *Either/Or*, this choice of ourselves is described as a double movement. B writes explicitly that the choice has two movements. The first one consists in an "isolation" where we separate ourselves from our world (3, 222; 240). The other consists in an identification, a return. The result of the first one is an abstract self. The other movement shows that the single individual is inseparable from his world. It is only here that we become, as B puts it, "concrete" (3, 229; 248).

The double movement is a form of repetition since we take back or rather are given back ourselves; we regain ourselves. The concept of repetition finds its fullest analysis in the book by the same name, *Repetition*, which was published 16 October 1843, the same day as *Fear and Trembling*. Kierkegaard repeatedly circles around this concept, and when he does, he often links repetition with freedom, as he does in *The Concept of Anxiety* (117 fn; 18 fn); especially in *The Concept of Anxiety* it becomes clear that the category *repetition* destroys the framework within which B reflects in *Either/Or*. This is already apparent in the distinction between a first and a second ethics, which is outlined in the preface of *The Concept of Anxiety* (and to which we will return later). Repetition is, as the preface of *The Concept of Anxiety* stresses, a religious category. Either existence in its entirety ends up in the requirement of ethics, which is the requirement of the first ethics, or existence starts all over again "through a transcendence. This transcendence separates repetition from the former existence /Tilværelse/ by such a chasm" (116 fn; 17f fn). The use of the word transcendence in this note means that which renews "the whole of life and of existence." It is redemption or freedom understood as a possibility coming from the outside, which *The Concept of Anxiety* discusses later.

Until now I have discussed the concept of freedom based on what B states in *Either/Or*. This constitutes the basis for what is stated later in Kierkegaard's writings, but, as we just indicated, some crucial shifts take place; this is especially the case in *The Concept of Anxiety*, which, in a certain sense, gives us a new starting point. The change in the later works consists first and foremost in that the understanding of unfreedom is further developed. Perdition is no longer just a particular way of living that the ethicist can have outside of himself. The problem of acknowledging ourselves, which has already been touched on in *Either/Or*, becomes critical in understanding the requirement of becoming ourselves. It is especially here that anxiety achieves its meaning, for the self-relation manifests itself as a problem in anxiety, since we can make ourselves unfree. I will return to this in a moment, but first we must examine whether freedom is automatically true freedom. When we know what true freedom is, is there anything more to say about freedom?

Freedom—and Freedom

Does freedom merge into true freedom? Even though Kierkegaard does not state it explicitly, he must presuppose another concept of freedom when he writes about true freedom. For true freedom is a freedom that first has to come into existence. A human being is faced with the task of becoming himself. This means that he must relate to this task or requirement, and in this lies the possibility of failing the task. An individual can fail, as Kierkegaard states it, by "losing himself." He can lose his freedom by what he does. When Kierkegaard writes of true freedom, the presupposition is therefore that a human being can relate in different ways to the task of becoming himself. But is not freedom being able to relate in different ways?

It is evident in *The Concept of Anxiety* that Kierkegaard also uses the word "freedom" in another sense than true freedom. As mentioned in *The Concept of Anxiety*, he writes of *the* freedom when he wants to indicate the meaning of anxiety. In a passage already quoted, it is stated that anxiety is freedom manifesting itself to itself in possibility. It is not only the possibility of freedom that manifests itself; it manifests itself to freedom itself. This freedom that is already there is, in a certain sense, the subject around which *The Concept of Anxiety* revolves. In another passage, Kierkegaard states that the entire book is about "freedom's psychological attitudes toward sin" (202; 118). Again we hear of *the* freedom but as a (human) *subject* that can make a decision or adopt a position. In both passages man is replaced by freedom. The possibility of freedom is manifested to the individual as a self that can relate to itself. The freedom that is already there thus consists in man already relating to himself.

This is developed in *Sickness unto Death* where Kierkegaard emphasizes that man is a synthesis or a relation in the sense that he relates to the relation that he is. It is "a relation that, even though it is derived, relates itself to itself, which is freedom. The self is freedom" (15, 87; 29). Here we are given a definition of what freedom is. To be sure, on a first reading he writes about what the self is ("The self is freedom"), but this provides us with an identification. The self means self-relation, to relate to ourselves, "which is freedom."

Thus freedom is not just to be in agreement with oneself. Freedom in the "true" sense of the word—as self-agreement—manifests itself as a task or a problem for the individual who is already posed in relation to himself. That a human being is already a self-relation must be understood this way: in what he does, man is doing something with himself. By relating to something, the individual also relates to himself; he brings himself along. In other words, freedom consists already in the self relating to itself since we are relating to ourselves.

In what sense can we talk of freedom here? Evidently it is not "true" freedom. While this freedom is a freedom in a normative sense as the task or the goal with which a human being is faced, we are now dealing with a freedom that we cannot escape even if we wanted to. It is a part of being a self. But it is not the unspecific freedom of choice either, where we freely and arbitrarily can choose between different possibilities. Of course, we are faced with a possibility, but it is precisely the critical possibility that we are determined in relation to, the good through which we become ourselves. In this sense there is only one thing to choose, the good. Since we are dealing with a choice, there is the possibility of not choosing the good, but the point is that we cannot do this indifferently; on the contrary, we become unfree.

Freedom in this other sense (other than true freedom) consists in choosing for ourselves. It does not rule out that in the choice we make, we are determined by our surroundings, but in so far as we are situated in relation to our surroundings, it is already implied that we do something ourselves. Since we relate to something we can relate differently. If we, for instance, have committed ourselves, we can refrain from fulfilling that commitment. We are already situated in relation to the person we have made a commitment to, and we can therefore be situated differently—we can pledge ourselves or we can withdraw our pledge. We can place ourselves in relation to that which we do or what other people expect us to do. Freedom is, in this case, the possibility of relating differently from the way we have done or do, or from what other people expect.

Unfreedom as a Phenomenon of Freedom

That we need an additional concept of freedom, besides true freedom, is clear from Kierkegaard's description of unfreedom. Let us start "backwards," with *Sickness unto Death*. The sickness in the title is despair in the sense of not being ourselves. When Kierkegaard calls it a sickness, the idea is that it is a sickness with a particular essence. Despair is not only a state we fall into; the individual "is *bringing* it upon himself" (15, 76; 17). We can say that a human being brings a sickness upon himself, for instance by imprudence. When Kierkegaard italicizes the word, it is to make the difference stand out. Despair is something one brings upon oneself. We do not just bring it upon ourselves when we get the sickness, but we get it at every moment that we are in despair. In this sense, we are in despair "by our own doings." We are unfree in despair by making ourselves unfree.

This understanding of unfreedom was already articulated in *Philosophical Fragments*. As mentioned, *Philosophical Fragments* states that sin is to be in untruth by our own fault. It is explained in that we are "bound" by ourselves (6, 20; 16). The individual has "imprisoned himself, and no one is so dreadfully imprisoned, and no captivity is so impossible to break out of as that in which the individual holds himself captive" (6, 21f; 17).

This is elaborated in *The Concept of Anxiety*. Anxiety about evil and anxiety about the good are forms of unfreedom. I have touched on this in chapter 1, and thus I only need to quote the definition of the demonic: it is "unfreedom that wants to close itself off" (206; 123). The demonic "closes itself up within itself, and in this lies what is profound about existence (Tilværelsen), precisely that unfreedom makes itself a prisoner" (207; 124). We could then notice that the issue is unfreedom (not freedom), but freedom constitutes the foundation of unfreedom. *The Concept of Anxiety* talks about "freedom, which underlies unfreedom or is its ground" (206f; 123) and about "the freedom scuttled and sunk in unfreedom" (219; 137). And it is stated explicitly that "unfreedom is a phenomenon of freedom" (217 fn; 135 fn).

That unfreedom is a phenomenon of freedom must mean that freedom in one way or another manifests itself in unfreedom. The freedom in question is the freedom where the self relates to itself. When Kierkegaard in *Philosophical Fragments* writes about the individual being in untruth or unfreedom "solely by himself," it means that he is in unfreedom by his actions. He "uses the power of freedom in the service of unfreedom" (6, 21; 17), since he is "freely in it" (6, 21; 17). "The power of freedom" (6, 21; 17) means the self-relating self.

This also explains what kind of unfreedom Kierkegaard is interested in here. It is an unfreedom to which we chain ourselves. We are unfree since we relate unfreely—to ourselves.

When we speak about the freedom that consists in the self relating to itself, the phenomena of this freedom is characterized by the ambiguous possibility of anxiety. In the demonic enclosing reserve, ambiguity becomes fixed into two wills. The demonic is determined by that against which it closes itself up, and this is, according to Kierkegaard, the good, understood as redemption or salvation. We do not just find ourselves in this unfreedom, but keep ourselves in it. At the same time, we are affected by the possibility of freedom. The demonic inclosed person harbors the possibility, which he resists, of manifesting himself This possibility emerges as an impulse, almost as a spontaneous manifestation of life, since there is also another will in the demonically enclosed person, the one he restrains. He has "two wills, one subordinate and impotent that wills revelation and one stronger that wills inclosing reserve" (211; 129). The "freedom, which underlies unfreedom or is its ground," enters "into communication with freedom from without" (206f; 123) and by that it betrays unfreedom "in such a way that it is the individual who in anxiety betrays himself against his will" (206f; 123).

The freedom that underlies unfreedom is self-relating, but this freedom implies the possibility of manifesting ourselves. In the demonic enclosing reserve, the self-relation becomes unfree so that we oppose the possibility that, in fact, seems to be implied by self-relating, namely manifesting ourselves. But this self-relation manages to assert itself by the fact that, affected by the possibility of freedom ("into communication with freedom from without"), we happen to reveal ourselves involuntarily.

Since unfreedom is a phenomenon of freedom, freedom must manifest itself through unfreedom. The question was in what way. We have now been given the following answer: first, we are dealing with an unfreedom that we are in "freely," since we chain ourselves to it; second, this unfreedom is negatively determined in relation to the good that is or that makes us free. It is most apparent in the demonic enclosing reserve, which is deter-mined in opposition to the possibility of the good. The demonically enclosed person resists this possibility out of anxiety about the good, but he is then negatively linked to it—and to himself.

Thus freedom appears negatively in unfreedom. The question is if there is also a more positive relation between the experience of unfreedom and the understanding of freedom. Let us first take a closer look at Kierkegaard's description of the negative phenomena of unfreedom. As we have already shown, Kierkegaard primarily writes about unfreedom in connection to anxiety and despair.

CHAPTER 4

Anxiety and Despair

Sickness unto Death

Both the analysis of anxiety (chapter 1 above) and the understanding of human existence (chapter 2) pointed to the fact that a human being is a self who is faced with the task of becoming himself. It became apparent that the determination of the ethical in *Either/Or* had this task as its object: the fundamental choice is to choose ourselves, which means to become ourselves (chapter 3).

What is worth noting in *The Concept of Anxiety* is that we reach an understanding of man as a self through anxiety in which we are placed outside of ourselves and where we can see ourselves as a stranger. As mentioned, the ambiguous meaning of anxiety was this: it gives us the possibility of discovering ourselves as selves, but of us becoming unfree in anxiety, which in such an anxiety means that we are not ourselves.

This particular perception of man as a self, which *The Concept of Anxiety* examines in an indirect way, is more fully developed in *Sickness unto Death* (published in 1849). This work can be read as a treatise on man as a self. The book begins in a staccato rhythm with the claim that "a human being is spirit" only to be followed by the question, "But what is spirit?" The passage continues: "Spirit is the self. But what is the self?" This is the question that the book wants to answer. Or rather, we can go back to the question that is implicit in the very first sentence: what is man? This question, which does not need to be articulated, is the question of the whole book. The answer that the book wants to develop is, as mentioned, that man is a self.

The insight obtained through the analysis of anxiety is maintained in *Sickness unto Death*. Man is a synthesis or a relation between heterogeneous elements in such a way that the coherence between them is fragile. The self as the third means to relate to ourselves as to what is the heterogeneous, as soul and body, finite and infinite, temporal and eternal. The coherence between the heterogeneous elements is in this self-relation or is the self-relation. Thus the self is both to relate to ourselves and the coherence with ourselves (to be ourselves).

Here *Sickness unto Death* repeats the insight that, in particular, was articulated in the determination of what it means to exist. As a self, a human being is in process, "in the process of becoming," even in the process of becoming himself. In being a self lies the task of becoming ourselves.

These two insights—man as a synthesis who relates to himself and with the task of becoming himself—are summarized into something like a formula in this short passage from *Sickness unto Death*: "The self is the conscious synthesis of infinitude and finitude that relates itself to itself, whose task is to become itself" (15, 87; 29).

Again sounding like a formula, the text continues by explaining what it means to become ourselves: "To become oneself is to become concrete. But to become concrete is neither to become finite nor to become infinite, for that which is to become concrete is indeed a synthesis. Consequently, the progress of the becoming must be an infinite moving away from itself in the infinitizing of the self, and an infinite coming back to itself in the finitizing process" (15, 87f; 30). As previously mentioned, Kierkegaard plays on the meaning of the word "concrete": to become concrete is to grow together with ourselves, to heal. This consists in getting the heterogeneous to cohere—for what has to grow together already belongs together in a certain sense. We are dealing with factors in the relation: soul and body, finite and infinite. One cannot be without the other. A human being cannot be free of himself as somebody who is both finite and infinite. If he tries nonetheless the relation will fail, but this does not mean that he then becomes either infinite or finite. On the contrary, the other factor is not left behind; it revenges itself in such a way so that the factor that is stressed is itself distorted.

Now, almost unintentionally, I have brought up the negative, that the relation fails. However, it is worth noting that the passage concerns the relation that succeeds. The passage outlines what it means to become concrete: "an infinite moving away from itself in the infinitizing of the self, and an infinite coming back to itself in the finitizing process." "The progress of the becoming" thus consists of a double movement that repeats itself in different variations, as in the formulation in *Either/Or* that we have already touched on. To become ourselves demands a separation from ourselves and means to return to ourselves or to come "back to ourselves" in the sense: to find ourselves.

Thus the passage I quoted tries positively to outline what it means to become ourselves. However, the continuation of the passage reads, "But if the self does not become itself, it is in despair, whether it knows that or not" (15, 88; 30). This is no innocent remark. It actually states the central theme of *Sickness unto Death*. Even though the book, based on the opening question, was supposed to be a treatise about man as a self, it becomes a treatise about despair. This is precisely what the title of the book refers to. "Sickness unto Death" is, as the heading of part 1 or the first half of the book states it, despair. And despair is, as the continuation of the quoted passage indicates, not becoming ourselves or not wanting to be ourselves. Consequently we are back in unfreedom, whereby the connection to the analysis of anxiety becomes even more striking.

Consciousness and Will

According to Kierkegaard, despair means not to be ourselves. He differentiates between three basic forms of despair: first, the despair that is ignorant of being despair; second, in despair not to will to be oneself; third, in despair to will to be oneself. These definitions show that *knowledge* (*consciousness*) as well as *will* become crucial but also problematic aspects.

If we take the last form first, to be sure, despair is not to be ourselves, but this is apparently a question of will, although not in the sense that it is in our power to be or not to be ourselves. By "will," Kierkegaard does not understand having power over ourselves or being master over what we want. Our will is simply that which we will, and here it is possible that we do not want to be ourselves. If we accept this, we can, however, be surprised at the third form: in despair to will to be oneself. What is this supposed to mean? Is not wanting to be ourselves good? Certainly, but here the will manifests itself as a complicated relation, or rather self-relation. For we can want ourselves to be somebody that we are not. Our will could then mean that we want to have power over ourselves and control ourselves, which precisely is despair, since we would then not be ourselves. We cannot accept ourselves as the person we are, but we must become somebody else before we can accept ourselves.

I will return later to the second and third form of despair, not to will to be oneself and to will to be oneself, which are respectively the despair of weakness and of defiance. Let us look at the first form, the despair "not to be conscious of having a self"

(15, 73; 13). We can ask ourselves if this is despair. In a parenthesis that follows the passage quoted, Kierkegaard says that this despair is "not despair in the strict sense", because despair seems to require that we know that we are in despair. Thus Kierkegaard needs to have another determination of despair in reserve in order to speak about despair; this determination is that despair is a misrelation, namely in the self-relation. Or, despair is that the self-relation is a misrelation, or in other words, that we are not ourselves. When Kierkegaard, nonetheless, claims that this despair is a despair even though we are not conscious of it, it must be because there is also here a misrelation: a human being *is* already a self, but in the despair that is not despair in the strict sense, he is not conscious of having a self.

However, on closer examination things are even more complicated. According to the previous statements, it appears as if despair, to Kierkegaard, is not so much a question about whether we feel despair. Despair means that we are not ourselves. But this opens up the following objection: since such a misrelation is precisely in the self-relation, we must experience it ourselves— and is this not to feel despair?

The further complication is implied in that the misrelation can also consist in the consciousness of ourselves and in particular in the self-consciousness that we express. Kierkegaard's radical claim is that despair is a common state. In *Sickness unto Death*, the central passage in this context carries the title "The Universality of this Sickness (Despair)" (15, 81; 22). This touches on the question with which I ended chapter 1: in what sense is anxiety a part of a human being's life? On a first reading, there seems to be a difference from chapter 1: we are now unequivocally dealing with forms of unfreedom. But already in *The Concept of Anxiety*, Kierkegaard claimed that the demonic "covers a much larger field than is commonly assumed" (205;

122), and even that traces of the demonic can be found in every human being (206; 122). And in the chapter in *Sickness unto Death* that we just mentioned, Kierkegaard refers to the anxiety that can turn into "an anxiety about oneself."

> Just as a physician might say that there very likely is not one single living human being who is completely healthy, so anyone who really knows mankind might say that there is not one single living human being who does not despair a little, who does not secretly harbor an unrest, an inner strife, a disharmony, an anxiety about an unknown something or a something he does not even dare to try to know, an anxiety about some possibility in existence or an anxiety about himself, so that, just as the physician speaks of going around with an illness in the body, he walks around with a sickness, carries around a sickness of the spirit that signals its presence at rare intervals in and through an anxiety he cannot explain. (15, 81; 22)

I have here quoted the beginning of the chapter about the universality of despair. If we further explore this chapter, we realize that Kierkegaard makes not one but two assertions. The first one is that despair is so ordinary that there is no single human being who, understood correctly, does not despair a little. The second assertion, intended to back up the first, states that not seeing ourselves as in despair is also a form of despair, whereby "thousands and thousands and millions" are placed in the category of despair (15, 82; 23). Thus the second assertion refers to the despair that is not despair in the strict sense of despair, which is not to be conscious of being in despair. The discussion about the "universality" of despair is hereby given a polemic tone. The idea is not only that every human being despairs a little or has traces of the demonic. The universality also turns out to mean that despair makes itself unremarkable or ordinary.

The crucial step that Kierkegaard takes here consists in examining what we ordinarily say about ourselves. It may be a shocking assertion that despair is supposed to be such an ordinary state that no man can deny that he is free of it. Kierkegaard's starting point is precisely that the individual is busy getting rid of or clear of despair. Consequently, Kierkegaard not only asks whether a human being feels that he is in despair. He takes notice of what the individual *says* about himself—about being in despair or not. What the individual says not only means what he tells other people about himself, but what he tells himself. In Danish we have this figure of speech: "*Det kan du sige dig selv*," which translates into something like "It is as plain as the nose on your face." The Danish figure of speech implies this: if you thought it through, the conclusion would be evident. But in fact a human being says something to himself, and he also says something to himself by what he tells other people.

Despair as a sickness of the spirit or self-relation has a "dialectical" character. The customary view "assumes that every man must himself know best whether he is in despair or not" (15, 81; 22). But such knowledge about ourselves is not simple. To know within ourselves what we are is to know of ourselves, to acknowledge ourselves, and in this knowledge lies the question of will: whether we want to know of ourselves. In addition, the situation is not just that on one side we have what a human being is, and on the other side what this human being says about himself. What a human being says is linked to his way of being. If a human being says that he is free of despair, there is good reason to be suspicious: when he says that he is free of despair, he does something about himself: he safeguards or assures himself, and in this way he can keep the unrest or anxiety at a distance.

This provides a change in the way Kierkegaard speaks of the "universality" of despair. Now the point is not only that every individual despairs a little, since deep within a human being lies an anxiety for something unknown and thus with traces of the demonic. What Kierkegaard describes is a way of living where the individual tries to hide this anxiety. Since the safeguarding or the assurance becomes the dominating characteristic of this way of living, it is determined even more so by anxiety. Anxiety hides in tranquility. "The physician of souls will certainly agree with me that, on the whole, most men live without ever becoming conscious of being destined as spirit— hence all the so-called security, contentment of life, etc., which is simply despair" (15, 85; 26). What is at issue here is a way of living that makes itself ordinary. In Kierkegaard's diagnosis of his own time, he calls such a way of living that believes itself to be ordinary the philistine-bourgeois mentality. Later in *Sickness unto Death* we read that "the philistine-bourgeois mentality is spiritlessness" (15, 97; 41). And "the anxiety that characterizes spiritlessness is recognized precisely by its spiritless sense of security" (15, 100; 44).

That we, nonetheless, are dealing with an anxiety in spiritlessness is because it is determined as an evasion. In anxiety we are evasive by safeguarding ourselves, but that which we evade is anxiety understood as the unrest deep within ourselves. Thus the anxiety of spiritlessness is an "anxiety of anxiety."

When Kierkegaard writes about the anxiety of spirit-lessness, we must differentiate between anxiety for something unknown that is deep within every human being, and someone seeking to safeguard himself against this anxiety by making himself ordinary. The attitude the individual takes towards anxiety, which can break through suddenly or gradually, creates the difference between the first with a trace of the demonic enclosing reserve, and the second with the issue of the philistine-bourgeois mentality and spiritlessness. In the first case, the anxiety or unrest manifests the possibility of freedom. By contrast, in spiritlessness the individual seeks to evade this possibility that is a difficult task: to become a self. He is evasive by not being conscious of being in despair.

Already the absence of consciousness of being in despair is thus problematic, but in the further analysis of the two other forms of despair (despair in the strict sense), the difference in consciousness becomes critical. By this difference in consciousness Kierkegaard can outline a course of different forms that despair can take.

Infinitude's Despair and Finitude's Despair

However, before making this outline Kierkegaard provides us with a structural description of the forms of despair. Since despair is a misrelation, it can be described by means of an account of what terms stand in the misrelation. Here the synthesis-definitions are displayed implicitly or negatively. We are dealing with, so to speak, the keyboard that despair uses in its concrete forms. This refers to the previous formulation about what it means to grow together with ourselves: infinitely to stray from ourselves in the infinitizing of the self and infinitely to come to ourselves in the finitizing process. When this development or movement fails, then either the infinitude or finitude is emphasized.

From the headings on the two sections where Kierkegaard describes the despair of infinitude and that of finitude, it is evident that the coherence in the relation also manifests itself in the negative: "Infinitude's Despair Is to Lack Finitude" and "Finitude's Despair Is to Lack Infinitude." The individual is already a relation between the finite and the infinite. When we fail to make this heterogeneous relation cohere, the coherence is manifested negatively.

Of what does infinitude's despair then consist? Here there are two key concepts: imagination and possibility. Imagination is, writes Kierkegaard, not an ability among other abilities, but fundamental, since imagination is "the medium for the process of infinitizing" (15, 88; 30). Imagination means the ability to see possibility (inasmuch as anxiety also concerns possibility, which, as we shall see, can even anticipate or evoke the possibility even though it is the negative, meaning the possibility of misfortune, we have a connection between anxiety and imagination). It is precisely the concept of possibility that is the second key concept. Infinitude's despair corresponds to the despair of possibility, as will be described later. Now, imagination or the ability to see possibility does not produce despair. However, there is the danger that we lose ourselves in imagination, or in the words of Kierkegaard we become "fantastic." "The fantastic is generally that which leads a person out into the infinite in such a way that it only leads him away from himself and thereby prevents him from coming back to himself" (15, 89; 31). In other words, the double movement of straying from ourselves and of returning to ourselves fails since we lose ourselves or run wild in the possibilities.

It is obvious that possibilities are an inseparable part of human life. It is because of the possibilities that the individual can find the air and space to acknowledge himself. Thus an open horizon of possibilities must be connected to this life. When we are young, life can seem like an infinite horizon of possibilities, with everything wide open to us, but this can also be a paralyzing experience. When we have grown older the horizon may seem reduced. But if the possibilities continue to be possibilities, if we have not determined ourselves in relation to them and actualized the possibilities that we have decided on, possibilities also become our destiny. The unredeemed possibilities become an essential part of our lives.

Even though Kierkegaard observes that in the despair of infinitude we lose ourselves and thus do not determine ourselves (or, using the expression from above, we do not return to ourselves), in this way a moment of fate can enter this despair. We will, so to speak, live in what we have not become.

Finitude's despair is to lack infinitude, or expressed in a parallel way, the despair of necessity is to lack possibility. But this is not in the sense that we feel it desperately. On the contrary, despair can go into hiding because we have adjusted ourselves to the given circumstances. Here despair consists in "having lost oneself, not by being volatilized in the infinite, but by being completely finitized, by becoming a number instead of a self, just one more man, just one more repetition of this everlasting *Einerlei*/one and the same/" (15, 91; 33). By this despair we let ourselves "be tricked out of /our/ self by "the others"" (ibid.). But this happens by giving up ourselves, whereby we will be able to "be going along superbly in business and social life, indeed, for making a great success in the world," "smooth as a rolling stone, as *courant* /passable/ as a circulating coin" (ibid.; 34).

What Kierkegaard here pins down is "the philistine-bourgeois" as expressed in the parallel description of necessity's despair. What is characteristic is that it is a despair that does not look like despair. Such a state is, according to Kierkegaard, spiritlessness. The philistine-bourgeois mentality lacks the imagination to see the misrelation; he lives "within a certain trivial compendium of experiences as to how things go, what is possible, what usually happens. In this way, the philistine-bourgeois has lost his self and God" (15, 97f; 41).

The Despair in Weakness and Defiance

The structural description of the different possible forms of despair (the despair of finitude and infinitude, the despair of necessity and possibility) constitutes the background for the analysis of the concrete forms that despair can take. Kierkegaard draws an ascending line starting from the despair that is not despair "in the strict sense," to a despair that in defiance asserts itself. A similar line is drawn in *The Concept of Anxiety*, and in both books the movement culminates in the demonic, the enclosing reserve. The defiant despair seems in fact to be an anxiety about the good.

I have already touched on the despair in which we do not know that we are in despair. When we do not know ourselves to be in despair, it is perhaps because we do not want to know that we are in despair or do not want to know of ourselves.

The next two basic forms of despair are the despair of weakness (in despair not to will to be oneself) and the despair of defiance (in despair to will to be oneself). However, weakness and defiance are ambiguous phenomena. In order to speak of despair there must be a resistance or defiance in weakness, and in the midst of defiance there must be a weakness. A human being who shows himself to be weak can be defiant or insist on his weakness, and the individual who displays defiance also displays weakness or dependency on what he is defiant about.

There is, however, an ascending movement from the despair of weakness to the despair of defiance, namely a growing consciousness of being in despair. And not only is an ascending line drawn from the despair of weakness to the despair of defiance, but there is also an intensification within the two basic forms.

Within the despair of weakness Kierkegaard differentiates between despair over the earthly or over something earthly on the one hand and despair of the eternal on the other hand. One would immediately say that we despair about what happens to us, especially when we lose something. This can be something specific: a job, wealth, a friendship, or maybe another human being. However, this is not despair, according to Kierkegaard. We may be able to acknowledge that, for instance, losing our financial support is not despair because that, after all, is an exterior circumstance of our life, but why do we not despair if we lose a loved one? Here Kierkegaard differentiates between despair and mourning. When we lose another human being we are supposed to mourn, but we are not supposed to despair. For despair concerns ourselves; despair means to give up ourselves or to be self-absorbed.

The point is not only that something specifically happens to us in the despair over "something earthly" and even over "the earthly." Despair can emerge from "one's capacity for reflection" (15, 110; 54). This means that the point is more to encounter something within ourselves that pushes us back, such as the lack of a specific talent. We can say that we are in despair over our life, but it is this life inasmuch as it is influenced by this lack (the lack of talent). The lack, or the loss that gives the occasion for despair, is given an infinite importance.

The next step to the despair of the eternal consists in that we are not only dealing with the despair of weakness but with being in despair over our weakness (15, 116; 60-61). Despair of the eternal is despair over and about ourselves. Kierkegaard is trying to create a difference of meaning in the prepositions: "We despair *over* that which binds us in despair—over a misfortune, over the earthly, over a capital loss, etc.—but we despair *of* that which, rightly understood, releases us from despair: of the eternal of salvation, of our own strength, etc." (15, 116 fn; 60f fn). We despair *over* that which causes despair, but we despair *of* that which despair concerns (like renouncing hope or courage).

It is not until this despair that we realize what despair is, namely "the loss of the eternal and of oneself" (15, 117; 62). In a single phase Kierkegaard writes about an increase of consciousness about what despair is and about the self (which here means consciousness about our own weakness).

The movement within the despair of weakness passes from a despair that is acted upon (where something happens to us) to a more acting despair (where we react to our own weakness), but we are still within a despair of weakness. In relation to this despair, the defiant or self-asserting despair is acting. We are dealing with a human being's attempt to "want to be master of itself or to create itself, to make his self into the self he wants to be" (15, 122; 68). It is not so much losing something or missing something as it is wanting to be ourselves—the way we want to be. However, the defiant despair is also a despair that is acted upon, for when we want to be something other than what we are, it is because there is something about ourselves that we do not want to acknowledge, and from which we suffer. It is not until we have recreated ourselves that we will become ourselves. But we are already "this very specific being with these natural capacities, predispositions, etc. in this specific concretion of relations, etc." (ibid.; 68).

So, we also encounter ourselves in the more defiant despair. We encounter some difficulty, a basic defect (*grundskade*, 11, 250; 269) within ourselves that we do not want to acknowledge. We can then become obsessed with the basic defect and in defiance assert ourselves through this basic defect. In this sense we will also despairingly be ourselves. This means that we will not be free of the basic defect. We suffer by our own doings, but we want this suffering at the same time. In this way the consciousness of ourselves is intensified, and the more intensified it gets the more despair is potentiated to become the "demonic" (15, 126; 72). We must observe that in *Sickness unto Death* the demonic is given a more intensified meaning than in *The Concept of Anxiety*. The demonically enclosed person now insists on his agony. While it was stated in *The Concept of Anxiety* that there are traces of the demonic in every individual, Kierkegaard now states that the demonic despair is rarely seen in the world (ibid.).

Thus the description of despair stretches from the despair where the person is ignorant of being in despair, to in despair not to will to be himself, and ends with the defiant despair to will to be himself, or rather it ends with the most potentiated form, the demonic despair. It is a movement from a despair that in fact lacks inwardness to a continually potentiated enclosing reserve where inwardness in the end has reached an impasse. As in *The Concept of Anxiety*, Kierkegaard outlines a movement that reaches the enclosing reserve where inwardness disappears (223; 141) or is distorted. This differentiation between the enclosing reserve and inwardness seems to mean that inwardness must be able to manifest itself (in order to remain inwardness). As with the anxiety about the good, the demonic despair turns in defiance against the possibility of goodness. "In hatred toward existence, it wills to be itself, wills to be itself in accordance with its misery" (15, 127; 73).

Ambiguity and Double-mindedness

From the beginning of this book I have stressed the way in which Kierkegaard poses his questions about anxiety: what does anxiety reveal about being a human being? Anxiety indicates that a human being is a wondrously constituted entity, an "intermediate being" between animal and angel. He is a being with an ambiguous possibility, the possibility of freedom, and anxiety itself is an ambiguous power, a foreign power, and yet it is man himself. Anxiety even means to relate ambiguously. This ambiguous way of relating comes out in the demonic as a split between two wills, a self-contradiction.

It is possible to expand the description of ambiguity. To relate ambiguously also means more explicitly to have reservations about our actions, or to want something without fully wanting it. Already in *Either/Or* Kierkegaard describes depression as "the sin of not willing deeply and inwardly, and this is a mother of all sins" (3, 177; 189). Prior to this passage, B explains that we are dealing with an interrupted movement. "As immediate spirit, a person is bound up with all the earthly life, and now spirit wants to gather itself together out of this dispersion, so to speak." Depression occurs when the movement to "gather itself together out of this dispersion, so to speak, and to transfigure itself in itself" is stopped (ibid.; 188-89). As he does later in *Sickness unto Death*, Kierkegaard describes a movement that fails, the movement of gaining continuity with ourselves. The task is to find coherence in our life that time disperses. In *Either/Or* the description of depression is a description of despair, but in this book despair is understood as letting our life be absorbed by or letting it depend on that which changes, and thus as a more or less hidden despair over a threatening nothingness. Here depression is the basic form of despair. And in depression there is anxiety, since it stops something or holds something down that would like to get out, namely spirit or the gaining of clarity about ourselves; the spirit wants the individual "consciously to possess himself" (3, 175; 186).

Depression can indirectly be described as double-mindedness, for we want something and yet we do not fully or "deeply and inwardly" want it. Kierkegaard describes double-mindedness more explicitly in other contexts, first and foremost in part 1 of *Upbuilding Discourses in Various Spirits* published in March 1847. Its heading is "An Occasional Discourse." This is a speech given on the occasion of a confession. The speech that concerns gathering ourselves together has as its major theme to will only one thing. However, the theme is developed negatively by describing different forms of double-mindedness, being of two minds and thus not willing only one thing. First, though, Kierkegaard states that willing only one thing is willing the good where, once again, the good is understood as that which gives coherence and that which enables us to acknowledge ourselves. Of course we could ask if it is not possible for the individual to will evil as one thing. The description of the demonic answers this in a sense. Evil is determined as resistance, revolt, and thus as a dual or double-minded will.

Let us return to the description of double-mindedness. Here we are not dealing with wanting evil but exactly the opposite: more or less, to a certain degree wanting the good. We want it, with reservations, without fully wanting it. Kierkegaard differentiates between different forms of double-mindedness: we can want the good for what we get out of it (for our reward); we can want it out of fear of punishment; or we can want it so that it must prevail with our aid whereby we use the good to assert ourselves. In these three forms we may want the good, but we also want something else. Kierkegaard mentions a fourth form, which is wanting the good to a certain degree. This is, in fact, not an independent form of double-mindedness, but the basic form. Double-mindedness is, as mentioned, wanting the good to a certain degree, meaning without fully wanting it even though the good is precisely that which we can want fully. Such a double-mindedness can manifest itself in busyness where there is no time or tranquility for gathering ourselves together. Even though we may feel like a victim of busyness while, nonetheless, seeking it, busyness can, in fact, be a way of keeping the task at a distance. Double-mindedness can, for example, also express itself in a feeling for the good where we do not go beyond the feeling.

In *Upbuilding Discourses in Various Spirits*, Kierkegaard identifies despair with double-mindedness: "or is not despair /fortvivlelse/ actually double-mindedness /tvesindethed/; or what else is it to despair but to have two wills!" (11, 35; 30). This means, on the other hand, that in double-mindedness we make ourselves unfree—we are precisely not ourselves.

Again, it is possible to expand the description of double-mindedness. For double-mindedness manifests itself in the relationship to the other person to whom we should do good. In *Works of Love* from September 1847, Kierkegaard again pays attention to the negative phenomena. Or rather to how love can change, i.e., become something other than love. Once again he begins with anxiety, for an anxiety hides in the spontaneous love. This sounds strange since we would not link anxiety to a spontaneous love that is happy and indescribably confident (12, 34; 29), a seeming contradiction that Kierkegaard himself observes. However, it is an anxiety for the possibility of change, meaning the possibility that love ceases (12, 38; 33). In the spontaneous love that is not more spontaneous than we are aware of its being spontaneous, we relate to this possibility in a more or less concealed way. Anxiety or unrest can manifest itself when lovers feel a need to make a greater commitment.

Kierkegaard elaborates on the possibility of change (12, 39ff; 34-35). Love is changed *within* itself in hatred, while passion is precisely maintained. Love is in jealousy[1]—full of anxiety—changed also within itself. When love becomes a habit, however, it is changed *from* itself since passion disappears. As a recurrent possibility, Kierkegaard describes the look of comparison through which we evaluate the other person according to what he deserves, or by comparing his actions to ours. In envy this comparison can become a sickness, whereby the mutual relation becomes nothing more than evaluation and comparison. Again Kierkegaard speaks about making ourselves unfree. We chain ourselves to the evaluation of the other, and envy almost ends up being the occasion itself.

To what extent do these phenomena refer to double-mindedness? Fundamentally they show the possibility of being in a relationship with another human being where we, at the same time, have a reservation in such a way that we place ourselves outside of the relationship, and thus we make it ambiguous. Yet, this reservation may not exactly be what we are dealing with in jealousy (zea-sickness). In jealousy (zea-sickness), we are almost absorbed in the relationship. Nonetheless, the reservation is apparent in jealousy (zea-sickness) where love burns, but it burns doubly or is fueled by itself. As for habit, we

---

[1] Arne Grøn uses first the Danish word *iversyge* and then, in parenthesis, *jealousy*. Howard and Edna Hong translate in *Works of Love*, page 35, these words by "zeal-sickness" and "jealousy" respectively. However, since "jealousy" is the best translation in this context I have decided to use the word "jealousy." To indicate when Arne Grøn otherwise uses the Danish word *iversyge*, I write "zeal-sickness" in parentheses. Trans.

can ask if love is still present. Here the reservation, meaning wanting to a certain degree, has become the way we relate and yet habit can pretend to be love. In comparison we can very well pretend to want the good. Comparison can be the way in which the reservation works. However, when it comes to hatred, the issue is not so much the reservation of the double-mindedness to do good as the resistance that makes double-mindedness into two wills.

Self-Encircling Phenomena

The phenomena here described, the different forms of anxiety, despair, and double-mindedness, are negative in the sense that they consist in a particular form of unfreedom. What characterizes these phenomena is that the individual makes himself unfree, that he imprisons himself. Using another expression, we can describe these phenomena as self-encircling around themselves. For example, it is evident with jealousy (zeal-sickness) or envy; the latter can explicitly be characterized by being "fueled by itself." It nourishes itself. It is even more evident with the demonic enclosing reserve where the will explicitly revolves around itself. It is perhaps less evident with the double-mindedness that consists of having a reservation about what we do so that we make it ambiguous. But Kierkegaard himself traced despair back to double-mindedness of wanting without wanting fully. In double-mindedness we are not in agreement with ourselves, and in this sense we are in despair.

Now the obvious question is what is the counterpart to the self-encircling phenomena. Firstly, we must be faithful to what Kierkegaard indicates himself: that which saves a person from the enclosing reserve is the word or language, the communication where we participate in a community. Simple-mindedness or simplicity is put up against double-mindedness, but simplicity is not understood as immediacy; it is understood as wanting only one thing, to be of one mind in what we do. That which cancels double-mindedness in the relationship to the other person is love, not so much as an act of will as an impulse that already exists, which God has "bestowed upon" us and that we will have to rediscover. Faith is determined as the direct counterpart to anxiety as well as despair. Later in the book I will have an occasion to return to this.

Secondly, I want to argue that the strength of the description of negative phenomena, the "negative phenomenology" that I have outlined, is that the counterpart can be extricated from the phenomena themselves. We understand what freedom is through the description of what unfreedom is. The negative phenomena are ethically determined. This is not only evident from the description of anxiety about evil and anxiety about the good, or from the description of despair not to will to be oneself. But also the double-mindedness is described as wanting the good with two minds. From another perspective, the reservation of double-mindedness can be described like this: we do not let ourselves be committed to what we see, nonetheless, as the good.

Does the foregoing give a more specific answer to the question about the meaning of anxiety? Why does a human being have to learn what it is to be in anxiety?

CHAPTER 5

To Lose Oneself—and to Win Oneself

Anxiety and Despair: The Possibility of Freedom?

As mentioned, the question for Kierkegaard is the meaning of anxiety, what anxiety reveals specifically about being a human being. First we are given the answer that anxiety reveals that a human being is a wondrously constituted being, a synthesis. This Kierkegaard further specified by stating that a human being is a self that is faced with the task of becoming himself. Then it was revealed that anxiety itself has an ambiguous meaning: a human being must free himself from anxiety, but he must also learn what it means to be in anxiety. Why this ambiguous meaning?

In the previous chapter I connected the analysis of anxiety to Kierkegaard's description of other negative phenomena, first and foremost despair. Kierkegaard outlines an ascending movement in both the description of anxiety and the description of despair, and in both cases this movement ends up in the demonic enclosing reserve. In addition, the anxiety about evil even seems to correspond to the despair of weakness (i.e., that which cannot be free of evil), and the anxiety about the good seems to correspond with the despair in defiance (i.e., that which cannot be free of the good [11, 35; 30]). But is there not also a difference?

Kierkegaard not only outlines two parallel courses, for the analysis of despair refers to anxiety. This comes out in the description of the despair that is ignorant of being despair. Here anxiety reveals that we are dealing with despair. On the other hand, *The Concept of Anxiety* seems to end in a description of anxiety as despair, first and foremost in the demonic enclosing reserve. If we state this to the extreme, then anxiety enters at the beginning of the analysis of despair, while despair is the result of the analysis of anxiety.

We can then ask if anxiety is, in fact, a negative phenomenon. There seems to be this critical difference between anxiety and despair: anxiety is more than a phenomenon of unfreedom; it is also the possibility of freedom. Fundamentally, anxiety means the possibility of discovering ourselves as a self that must relate to himself. In a sense we can claim that the analysis of anxiety comes before the analysis of despair, since it shows the possibility of discovering the self-relation as the presupposition in the determination of despair (understood as a misrelation in the self-relation). Despair, on the contrary, seems fixed in the negative meaning: not to be ourselves. While anxiety is ambiguous (with both the possibility of freedom and unfreedom), despair seems more unequivocally to be a negative phenomenon.

But is this in fact true? Already in *Either/Or*, B states that the people "whose souls do not know this depression are those whose souls have no presentiment of a metamorphosis" (3, 178; 190). And in *Sickness unto Death* the question is posed whether despair is an asset or a defect. The answer is that "purely dialectically, it is both." It is clear that it is a defect, but it also contains an asset that is even infinite. "The possibility of this sickness is man's superiority over the animal" (15, 74; 15). In a similar way, even if it is more unequivocal, Kierkegaard states in *The Concept of Anxiety* that anxiety is not an imperfection in man (145; 52), but it is an expression, on the contrary, of the perfection of human nature (162; 72). We can add to this the shared feature of the analysis of anxiety and despair that those who claim to be free of anxiety and despair can be declared without spirit. Also, those who claim to be free of despair have not discovered themselves as a self. The only way to be free of despair is by freeing ourselves, that is to say to go through despair. A human being also seems to have to learn what it means to despair. It is not only anxiety that provides the possibility of getting to know ourselves as a self; despair does this too. When an individual needs to learn to be anxious or to be in despair, it is because both anxiety and despair can conceal themselves and because it is important to understand both anxiety and despair in the right way.

The analysis of anxiety and the analysis of despair coincide in the understanding of unfreedom. The individual makes himself unfree; he "loses himself." At the same time the aim in the analysis is the same: as a self, the individual is faced with the task of becoming himself, and he becomes himself by growing together with himself, to win himself. Kierkegaard links this in an evangelically influenced formula: to lose ourselves in order to win ourselves. But in what sense must a human being lose himself in order to become himself?

A Detour through the Negative

If the negative means that it is necessary to go through it in order to be free, it is critical to know this: in what sense negative?

In different ways I have stressed the meaning of the negative. It stretches from the admitting of ignorance of what it means to be a human being as the starting point for being able to pose the question (chapter 2) to unfreedom understood as not being ourselves. It is worth noticing that when Kierkegaard speaks about freedom or becoming ourselves, he speaks of unfreedom or not being ourselves. *The Concept of Anxiety*, as a treatise on freedom, has anxiety as its central point not only as trapped or bound freedom, but as unfreedom, and *Sickness unto Death* as a treatise on the self is an analysis of despair about not being ourselves. Is there a point in making this detour?

First, freedom is given its meaning by canceling unfreedom. The difficulty of explaining true positive freedom is linked to the fact that this freedom is an answer to experiences of unfreedom where we make ourselves unfree. Freedom must contain an understanding of what this unfreedom means.

Second, becoming ourselves seems to demand that we "lose ourselves." In *Sickness unto Death*, Kierkegaard expresses it this way: "The self must be broken in order to become itself" (15, 120; 65). The self must—by means of the eternal—have "the courage to lose itself in order to win itself" (15, 122; 67). It is implied in the unfreedom of anxiety and despair that we resist getting to know ourselves. This resistance need not be apparent. Refusing to acknowledge ourselves often manifests itself in that we precisely think we know who we are. We can think this in the comfort of being ordinary or in defiance. In the latter case we create ourselves according to our own conception. We want to be in control of ourselves, be our "own master" (15, 123; 69). That the self "is broken" then means that this conception we have about ourselves is broken. We are actually thrown back on ourselves. Thus to become ourselves demands that we "lose ourselves" as the person we thought or imagined we were. Here the expression from *Either/Or* is given an intensified meaning: to become ourselves demands that we receive ourselves. We first have to get to know ourselves—again.

So how are we required to lose ourselves? It is important to distinguish between two senses of losing ourselves (meaning not only losing our self). First of all it means to slip out of one's hands. Second, we can lose ourselves since we can make ourselves unfree. We lose ourselves then by what we do. For example, this can consist in losing ourselves in our conceptions about what we are to become—in order to become ourselves, or that we forget ourselves in order "to be like the others" (15, 91; 34). When in this second sense of losing ourselves we have "lost ourselves," it is necessary to have the experience of not being in control of ourselves. To become ourselves is to grow together with ourselves and, through this, to get to know ourselves again. This demands that we "lose ourselves" in the first sense of losing ourselves: to admit that we have slipped out of our own hands—exactly by what we have done.

Most often Kierkegaard speaks about losing ourselves in the second sense. For instance, as can be seen in the following passage from *Sickness unto Death*, "The greatest hazard of all, losing the self, can occur very quietly in the world, as if it were nothing at all. No other loss can occur so quietly; any other loss—an arm, a leg, five dollars, a wife, etc.—is sure to be noticed" (15, 90; 32-33).

To lose ourselves is the greatest danger. Here we are apparently dealing with the second sense: to lose ourselves by what we do ourselves. We lose precisely that, ourselves. Kierkegaard often uses the words from the Gospel of Matthew 16:26: "For what is a man profited, if he shall gain the whole world, and lose his own soul?" To lose ourselves is to wound our soul, and this means to harden ourselves so that we give up courage and hope. We do precisely something with ourselves— we give up (on) ourselves. As we have already seen, Kierkegaard emphasizes that this self-abandonment can very well be conceived in conjunction with achieving success and "gaining the whole world." He even links the two so that maybe the reward is bought precisely by losing ourselves. As we have already seen, self-abandonment can be unremarkable or make itself unnoticeable, even in such a way so that the loss leaves no mark on us. That which we forget is precisely that which anxiety reveals: that we are a self with the task of becoming ourselves. That which we give up is thus being faced with the task, but inasmuch as being a self is to be in process with the task, we give up being a self. This is what Kierkegaard calls spiritlessness.

To lose ourselves in the first sense is, however, to become aware of ourselves. But that we only become free by slipping out our own hands must also be due to the fact that freedom itself, as we shall see momentarily, ends up consisting in self-devotion.

From the beginning the question has been what anxiety reveals about being a human being. Until now the analysis has been dealing with man as a single individual. What it means to be a human being we only know individually and we become a self individually. But does the individual not also become a self in relation to other people? The description of the negative phenomena such as the enclosing reserve, jealousy (zeal-sickness), and envy could already indicate this.

CHAPTER 6

History

In *The Concept of Anxiety* we read, "The most profound reason for this is what is essential to human existence: that man is *individuum* and as such simultaneously himself and the whole race" (124; 28). "This" refers to the fact that the explanation of hereditary sin that places Adam "fantastically outside," namely outside "The history of the human race" (122; 25) is not helpful. That this explanation is not helpful is simply due to the fact that "every individual is both himself and the race" (185; 98). There is good reason to examine further this sentence that states "what is essential to human existence."

Kierkegaard's rejection of the notion of an unspecific freedom of choice (*liberum arbitrium*) had, as we saw in chapter 4, the point that the individual, who is to choose, is always posed in a specific way in a given context. The individual has a personal history. It manifests itself in that choosing ourselves, as the ethicist in *Either/Or* emphasizes, ends up meaning to repent, and it is implied that by repenting we appropriate our own history, the history that stretches all the way back through the history of the race.

That the individual in a significant sense has a personal history is stated more explicitly in *Either/Or*. The individual who chooses himself "discovers that the self he chooses has a boundless multiplicity within itself inasmuch as it has a history, a history in which he acknowledges identity within himself. This history is of a different kind, for in this history he stands in relation to other individuals in the race and to the whole race, and this history contains painful things, and yet he is the person he is only through this history" (3, 200; 216). It is worth noticing the wording in this passage, since it anticipates a crucial coherence between history and identity. The individual is the person he is only *by* this history, and this history of the individual is a history *in which* he acknowledges the identity with himself (insofar as he chooses himself). In this history in which the individual finds himself, he is in a relationship to other individuals and to the whole human race.

That the individual has a personal history is, as we have already seen, also emphasized in *The Concept of Anxiety*. "At every moment, the individual is both himself and the race. This is man's perfection viewed as a state. It is also a contradiction, but a contradiction is always the expression of a task, and a task is a movement, but a movement that as a task is the same as that to which the task is directed is an historical movement. Hence the individual has a history" (124f; 28f). That the individual not only has a personal history but purely and simply history, i.e., the individual is essentially his own history, is explained by saying that a contradiction is implied, a contradiction that as such is always an expression of a task.

Here we need to focus on the fundamental determination that the analysis of anxiety brought out: man is a synthesis. As we have seen, implied in this is that the individual is faced with the task of getting the heterogeneous aspects of himself to cohere. The heterogeneous, soul and body, is given a sharpened meaning in virtue of the sexual. Later in *The Concept of Anxiety* Kierkegaard states, "First in sexuality is the synthesis posited as a contradiction, but like every contradiction it is also a task, the history of which begins at that same moment" (142; 49). This is a wording that is similar to the previous passage.

The individual has a personal history, since he is faced with the task that is implied in being a synthesis. The individual's history begins at that same moment when the synthesis is posited as a contradiction, and this means at that same moment he becomes conscious of himself, or the coherence with himself, as a problem. The task is to be coherent with ourselves, or in other words to gain continuity or identity with ourselves. The individual's history is the history of the task (precisely as it was stated: as "a task, the history of which begins at that same moment"). We cannot understand what an individual is if we do not realize that we are faced with the task of gaining identity with ourselves, or in other words that it is a task for itself. This is supported by the determination that the analysis of existence brings out: that the individual is in process, in the process of becoming, and is even in the process of reaching himself, since he is to become himself.

Thus history as the individual's history is determined by the task of becoming oneself, and since Kierkegaard sees this task as the ethical, history is ethically determined. This may sound rather surprising, for it is a common perception that Kierkegaard cannot really attribute any meaning to history, and that, in any case, he puts the historical and the ethical in opposition to each other.

The opposition between the world-historical view and the ethical perspective is emphasized in *Concluding Unscientific Postscript* (for example, 9, 110ff, 133). Kierkegaard or Climacus finds the world-historical view ethically suspect because that view abstracts from the fact that the individual is an acting individual. When viewing the shared history as a history of the world, according to Climacus-Kierkegaard, the implication is that this history of the world has ended. It is over because it is stretched out before our eyes for us to view from the outside. Hence a necessity is attached to history that is not a part of history as experienced history. But the shared history can also be seen in a different way. In *Either/Or* the ethicist mentions the possibility of viewing it under the definition of freedom, that is to say to realize that "everything could be otherwise" (3, 164; 174). However, we can only understand this as an acting individual, meaning as an individual who has a history.

Here I would like to return to the earlier passage I quoted from *Either/Or*. In the history in which the individual acknowledges identity with himself, "he stands in relation to other individuals in the race and to the whole race" (3, 200; 216). In virtue of having a history *himself*, being in the process of becoming and thus being faced with the task of becoming himself, the individual is in a relationship with other individuals in the shared history. In other words, we have a shared history in virtue of the task that is shared in the sense that every single individual is faced with it.

Let us look at the way the other passage from above continues, the passage from *The Concept of Anxiety* that ended with the sentence "Hence the individual has a history." The passage continues like this: "but if the individual has a history, then the race also has a history" (125; 29). On a first reading this seems to get things the wrong way around. For it is a matter of course that the race has history, so much a matter of course that the individual's personal history seems to merge with the history of the race. Instead, the history of the race now seems to be understood through the individual's history. However, what is crucial is that the individual in his own history is linked to other individuals. "Each individual has the same perfection, and precisely because of this individuals do not fall apart from one another numerically any more than the concept of race is a phantom. Every individual is essentially interested in the history of all other individuals, and just as essentially as in his own" (125; 29). In virtue of having a history ourselves, by the task of gaining identity with ourselves, the individual is "essentially interested in the history of all other individuals." There is, in virtue of this task, this "same perfection," a shared history, and the understanding that this history opens up is in a sense an ethically determined understanding. The basic interest that we can have in knowing how other people live their lives and in reading accounts of these lives, can, of course, be explained as simple curiosity. But an inte-rest in achieving new knowledge about how life might have turned out and perhaps in being surprised at how different it is from our expectations leads us back, according to Kierkegaard, to the task with which each individual is faced: to shape his or her life.

Now, we might think that more is implied in the statements about the history of the race, because the individual does not have his history to himself; this history is determined by the history of the race. The individual is situated under the history of the race. In a sense this is implied in what was said earlier— most clearly when the ethicist in *Either/Or* speaks about how the individual must take on the history of the race by repenting. But, at the same time, it is implied that we make something our own by repenting. If we do not try to make our history our own, history becomes destiny. Thus, gaining identity with ourselves demands a form of separation from the history of the race.

However, this is supported by the fact that every individual starts all over again, in a place different from everyone else. In this sense the individual is already separated from the history of other individuals. The double coherence implied in the sentence that every individual is himself and the race all at once is articulated in the following passage: the idea is not to permit the individual "to play his little history in his own private theater unconcerned about the race. For the history of the race proceeds quietly on its course, and in this no individual begins at the same place as another, but every individual begins anew, and in the same moment he is at the place where he should begin in history" (130; 34f).

CHAPTER 7

The Single Individual and the Universally Human

Separation

Chapters 1 to 5 dealt with the human being as a single individual. This is evident from the two determinations with which we started. Anxiety distinguishes the single individual, and the problem of existence presents itself to the existing person (*den eksisterende*) as this particular individual. Individually we are human beings, or human beings individually. Furthermore, being a human being is determined by the task of becoming ourselves, and this happens by what Kierkegaard in other contexts calls "separation" (*udsondringen*). It is the separation from "the others."

The concept of the single individual is similarly given meaning in different contexts. In *The Concept of Anxiety* it is particularly linked to sin. Kierkegaard emphasizes that sin "enters into the single individual as the single individual" (143; 50); that is to say that "how sin came into the world, each man understands solely by himself" (144; 51). It is further stated that sin as category "is posited precisely in that the single individual himself, as the single individual, posits it" (149; 57) and that "the concepts of sin and guilt posit precisely the single individual as the single individual" (185; 98).

It is worth noticing the formula that is repeated: "the single individual *as the single individual*." In sin the single individual is "marked" as the single individual. Sin is a step the individual takes himself, and by taking this step the individual is distinguished as this single individual. One could then ask, in relation to what? The answer is, in relation to the whole world (185; 98). Now, the situation is not that the individual is simply placed before the world. A human being is, writes Kierkegaard, himself and the race all at once. "However, the concept of race is too abstract to allow the positing of so concrete a category as sin" (149; 57), for sin distinguishes the individual as this specific human being from other people.

As a treatise on sin or the different positions of freedom to sin (as previously stated), *The Concept of Anxiety* is about the distinguishing of the single individual as the single individual. It may be useful to examine the connection between sin and the single individual in Kierkegaard's books before and after *The Concept of Anxiety*.

In *Fear and Trembling* the concept of the single individual is designated vis-à-vis the ethical as the universal. Actually there are two distinctions. While *Either/Or* speaks about the ethical-religious, *Fear and Trembling* makes the radical step to distinguish the religious from the ethical. This happens by the single individual being distinguished from the universal. Hence the single individual is understood the other way round, as a religious category. The single individual is placed in relation to God who can speak to the single individual in such a way that he cannot communicate himself to other people. The universal is the ethical, but in this it is also speech or the shared language. However, it is viewed as something exterior in the sense that we express ourselves in language. Thus the central claim in *Fear and Trembling* is that the individual is "incommensurable" (5, 63; 63) with the exterior. A secret remains in each individual.

It is not entirely clear how this is to be understood. We can claim that not only the ability to communicate ourselves is part of being a person; it is a way of manifesting ourselves to others. But it is also something so basic that we can elude others in such a way that they cannot know us completely. Secrecy or concealment is also part of being a person. However, the assertion in *Fear and Trembling* seems to be that the single individual cannot actually communicate himself in the shared language without losing himself. The inner does not correspond to the outer.

If we jump from *Fear and Trembling* to *Concluding Unscientific Postscript*, we find that a remarkable shift has taken place. The issue is still the distinguishing of the single individual as the single individual. We can even say that it is the principal issue in *Concluding Unscientific Postscript*. It is particularly in this book that the expression "separation" is used. The single individual becomes a single individual by being separated from "the others," but this separation is now ethical. The ethical is no longer the universal outside of which the single individual is put. The concepts of the ethical and the single individual are so critically linked that the ethical is almost identical with the single individual becoming a single individual. I will return to this in the next chapter about the ethical. Before we get there, we must once more examine two key concepts: the single individual and the universal. In *The Concept of Anxiety*, the claim that the single individual is himself and the race all at once indicates that the single individual has the universal solely by himself, but, at the same time, the single individual seems to be determined as a single individual by distinguishing himself from the universal.

Becoming the Single Individual

Every human being is a single individual or the single individual. But, as mentioned, Kierkegaard adds this: the single individual *as* the single individual. This seems to mean that the single individual can be other than the single individual, or if we turn it around, the single individual *must become* the single individual.

Kierkegaard writes about the single individual in a more and more insistent tone, because more and more clearly he understands the danger that individuals, who are single individuals separately, with their own features, can become a crowd (*mængde*) or a mass of people (*masse*). However, the critical point is that this crowd or mass consists of individuals. The loss of independence that takes place is a loss for the single individual. Anonymity is a danger that exists for the single individual. When we speak about "the others," it is actually a possibility for the single individual to become a concept: letting ourselves be determined by the way we view others. The concrete others are separate individuals who perhaps also allow themselves to be determined by the way they view others. "The others" become an abstraction that we all share.

It is particularly this negative possibility of loss of self that creates the task of becoming a single individual. It is implied in this that we account for ourselves as this single individual, and thus we understand ourselves as this particular single individual.

In several places Kierkegaard has stressed the single individual as the category of his writings. In *Upbuilding Discourses in Various Spirits* from 1847, "that single individual" not only appears as the reader of the book in the preface of part 2. Part 1, the confessional address we mentioned earlier, is dedicated to "that single individual." Furthermore, the book is also about the task of "becoming the singular individual." Kierkegaard puts that single individual in direct opposition to being "among the crowd," whereby he "never became conscious of himself as the single individual" (11, 137; 151). Here the important point is that even though everybody is an individual for himself, the task is, nonetheless, to become the single individual, and that oneself becomes the individual, in other words becoming a single individual for oneself. The negative possibility is precisely that we do not discover ourselves as the single individual. Thus the essential difference lies in how we view ourselves.

Kierkegaard develops the determination *the single individual* particularly in "Two 'Notes' Concerning My Work as an Author." The two notes were given the title "The Single Individual" and were published posthumously in 1859 as a supplement to *On My Work as an Author*. In the notes Kierkegaard observes the following: "but every human being is indeed an individual human being," and he then adds that "every human being, unconditionally every human being, can be and should be an individual, should place his honor—but will also truly find his salvation—in being an individual" (18, 161; 117). Even though every human being is an individual human being, the question remains if "he still has not really become the single individual" (18, 162; 118). In this lies the negative possibility that we do not become the single individual. Kierkegaard speaks about escaping "into the crowd" and thus "cowardly" eluding "being the single individual" (18, 153; 108), but this is precisely something the single individual does!

Thus implicit in the determination *the single individual* is a demand to become the single individual we already are. However, this demand seems to be universal. What is the situation with the universal and with the ethical?

The Universal

In *Concluding Unscientific Postscript*, being a human being was determined by the fact that we—you and I and the third—are human beings individually. But is this not a universal condition—to be human beings individually? As mentioned, here

Climacus makes the ethical into the task with which each individual is faced. Existence and the ethical are linked so that the task is to exist ethically. Now the ethical means the separation of the single individual. Thus he states, "for existing ethically, it is an advantageous preliminary study to learn that the individual human being stands alone" (10, 28; 323).

"The ethical is and remains the highest task assigned to every human being" (9, 126; 151), Climacus writes, but he then adds that "the ethical is the eternal drawing of breath and in the midst of solitude the reconciling fellowship with every human being" (9, 126; 152). In what does this fellowship consist? Does the fellowship just mean being a human being individually?

Let us take a closer look at the concept of the universal. The fact is that a crucial change of meaning occurs in the course of Kierkegaard's writings. In *Either/Or* the universal partly means what commits one ethically, partly the social context that the individual is formed by. "To become ourselves" even means expressing the universal in the individual life.

As the universal is determined by the norms of collective human life, the exception is created that falls outside of this collective life, against the universal. First and foremost, we are dealing with the religious exception around which *Fear and Trembling* revolves.

However, in the later writings, Kierkegaard emphasizes a different notion of the universal. Here he writes about the universally human that resists the "differences"; that is to say, the differences that exist between people and that give a society occasion to evaluate who is the most important. The universally human does not depend on differences in, for example, talent or social position, and, ethically speaking, the universally human is the task that confronts each individual.

At the same time as Kierkegaard's critical diagnosis becomes more and more directed towards the mutual comparison and evaluation that makes collective human life into a fearful solidarity, the universally human is given an even more polemical meaning. The universal is no longer that outside of which the exception falls. On the contrary, the universally human is what captures the social exception. It is also implied in this that the concept of exception has changed. The exception is that which the fearful solidarity is united against and thus expels.

Sympathy and Compassion

"If an observer will only pay attention to himself, he will have enough with five men, five women, and ten children for the discovery of all possible states of the human soul" (209; 126). We can ponder why exactly ten children. Are the ten children in fact the five men and five women? Maybe we do not need that many men, women, or children? In any case, earlier in *The Concept of Anxiety* Kierkegaard has referred to the Latin sentence *unum noris omnes* (to know one is to know them all), and he specified that by the word *unum* we must understand the viewer himself, thus holding fast to "the one that is actually all" (168 fn 2; 79 fn 2).

In *The Concept of Anxiety* Kierkegaard has scattered various "stage directions" about the observer and the viewer who also plays his own tricks in the book. In a sense, the remarks are also directed to the reader. The essential thing seems to be stated in what we just quoted: we must "take care of ourselves," i.e., have a look at ourselves when we observe other people. This does not mean that the observer should "turn his look inwardly." On the contrary, what is important is to have awareness of the phenomena that life offers, but this demands that we are aware of ourselves, i.e., that we do not forget who we are when we are observing other people.

Implicit in this is that something universally human exists; human possibilities that we have in common unite the observer with men, women, and children. Consequently, every individual is "essentially interested" in the history of other people, as previously stated.

This is now stressed by what Kierkegaard states about the sympathy that the observer must have: "One must have sympathy. However, this sympathy is true only when one admits rightly and profoundly to oneself that what has happened to one human being can happen to all. Only then can one benefit both oneself and others. The physician at an insane asylum who is foolish enough to believe that he is eternally right and that his bit of reason is ensured against all injury in this life is in a sense wiser than the demented, but he is also more foolish, and surely he will not heal many" (146f; 54).

This is later elucidated by the demand required of compassion. Just as the question was "what sympathy do we need," the question is now "in what way must we be compassionate" (in between the lines: to the person who is suffering in relation to himself). In the sense in which compassion is "usually" used, compassion,

> so far from being a good to the sufferer, is rather a means of protecting one's own egotism. Not daring in the deeper sense to think about such things, one saves oneself by sympathy. Only when the sympathetic person in his compassion relates himself to the sufferer in such a way that he in the strictest sense understands that it is his own case that is in question, only when he knows how to identify himself with the sufferer in such

a way that when he fights for an explanation he is
fighting for himself, renouncing all thoughtlessness,
softness, and cowar-dice—only then does the sympathy
acquire significance... (203f; 120)

Conscience and Fear of People

The basic consciousness in man is, according to Kierkegaard in
Upbuilding Discourses in Various Spirits, the consciousness of being
a single individual (11, 123; 134). How does this consciousness
manifest itself? In a certain sense it already manifests itself in
anxiety. For in anxiety we are separated so that we are faced with
the task of becoming ourselves. The consciousness also manifests
itself when we are isolated or separated from a community. But
maybe this consciousness appears most distinctly when we
separate ourselves from ourselves, or when, in a direct way, we
relate to ourselves as someone we take a position towards or we
position ourselves in relation to. And this is what happens in
con-science. Or rather, conscience is actually the basic
consciousness of being a single individual, i.e., this particular
single individual. Conscience is my own relation to myself that
other people cannot replace. In this sense I separate myself from
myself in conscience by already being separated from other
people. Conscience is the knowledge we have within ourselves
or the consciousness we have of ourselves that we cannot escape
or shift. Thus Kierkegaard can write that "you and the
conscience are one; it knows everything you know, and it knows
that you know it" (11, 120; 131). What can happen is that a
human being "completely deafens his conscience," but
Kierkegaard adds, "his conscience, since he does not get rid of it;
it still is his or, rather, he belongs to it" (11, 118; 129). To
deafen his conscience is actually what we previously called
"hardening ourselves," which is something we do to ourselves.

Thus we are already positioned in relation to ourselves; we cannot escape this consciousness of ourselves that is conscience, and yet we can avoid listening to "the voice of conscience" (11, 118; 129). Avoiding this voice is easier when we listen to something else, when we state something else, or when we adopt what other people are saying.

Here Kierkegaard speaks about two kinds of fear. There is the sickness of not fearing what a person should fear, "the voice of conscience," and then there is the sickness of fearing what a person should not and ought not to fear. This sickness is "cravenness and servility and hypocrisy" (11, 48; 46). It is what Kierkegaard in other contexts calls "fear of people." Fear of people need not manifest itself in avoiding the company of other people. On the contrary, it manifests itself especially by engaging too easily in such company. Kierkegaard calls the first kind pernicious; the other one is, however, even worse. The first kind is defiance, obstinacy, while the other one is, as we heard, cowardice. However, are the two kinds related? For does the first kind need to be so openly defiant (that we defy the voice that tells us what we should do)? Can deafening the voice of conscience in fact be cowardice? So that we deafen it by adjusting ourselves, maybe not to other people, but to that which we are letting other people count as.

However, once again this shows negatively the coherence between being a single individual, on one's own, and the relationship to other people, defined by the universally human (understood as that which Kierkegaard calls the common task: to pay attention to ourselves, which is particularly true in our relationship to others). Does this coherence also manifest itself positively?

Language

In *The Concept of Anxiety* when Kierkegaard describes the demonic enclosing reserve, he gives language a crucial role as the positive counterpart. This we have touched on earlier. He writes, "Inclosing reserve is precisely muteness. Language, the word, is precisely what saves, what saves the individual from the empty abstraction of inclosing reserve" (207; 124). Just before this, Kierkegaard states that freedom is constantly "communicating" (*communicerende*), and, incidentally, that it is desirable if people grasp the religious sense of the word *with* (participation in the sacramental communion). Kierkegaard moves on to discuss is revelation (the possibility of good) and being revealed or disclosed (*åbenbar*). The demonic reveals itself unwillingly by being two wills at odds with each other, and the demonic reveals itself precisely by getting into "communication" with freedom as the good outside of ourselves. Similarly, it is stated here: "For language does indeed imply communication" (ibid.; 124).

We can ask if Kierkegaard, by "language," means spoken language. Is communication here a relationship to other people? Or is the religious sense of the word of such crucial importance that we not only must realize this sense, but maybe primarily realize *just* this sense? As indicated, Kierkegaard shows that the religious sense is of crucial importance. The demonic is defiance against the good or the salvation that is offered to man from the outside. But, at the same time, the whole context is human language. The sudden, unwilling revelation occurs when the demonic person "comes out with it," and the communication is an expression of "continuity" that not only means the single individual's continuity with himself, but also "continuity with the rest of human life" (212; 130).

Since communication lies in language, it is natural to understand "speaking" to mean letting ourselves be known: to speak is to speak out. But this is not automatically so. Kierkegaard's statement about language lying in communication refers to a resistance to letting ourselves be known. Such a resistance also manifests itself through language, and it even does this in various ways. In the demonic enclosing reserve, the resistance manifests itself by the manifestation happening unwillingly as a sudden break with what is otherwise being stated. And when Kierkegaard later, in *Sickness unto Death*, asserts that despair is "universal," he is precisely examining what a human being states about himself. But by what he states, he can try to hide himself— even from himself.

Thus speech also gives us the possibility of not manifesting ourselves. The next question is whether a human being can only manifest himself indirectly: by what he states, he expresses something that is not directly stated. Does communication not also demand silence?

Silence is evaluated in different ways in Kierkegaard's writings. In *Fear and Trembling* the ethical is identical with the requirement for revealedness while the religious is linked to the silence that places the individual outside the universal. However, in *The Concept of Anxiety*, communication is the bearer of the religious, the good as disclosure. Silence seems to become demonic. However, Kierkegaard does differentiate between the demonic enclosing reserve and the enclosing reserve that awaits the right time to be revealed or disclosed. That silence is in danger of having demonic features is also admitted in *Fear and Trembling*.

But the question that follows is if there is not also a significant silence in successful communication, a silence that refers to the secret that is a part of being a person. In any case, Kierkegaard stresses that we are human beings individually, each with his own personal history, and that this is the condition for us having a shared history.

CHAPTER 8

The Ethical

The Ethical Choice

The universally human refers to a task we all share: each individual is faced with the task of becoming a single individual. Kierkegaard calls this task *the ethical*. As previously mentioned, the ethical is the highest task that an individual can be faced with without that task demanding a particular talent and thus without discriminating between people. Also in this sense it is a universal task. But on a first reading it may sound strange that becoming oneself, a single individual, is supposed to be the ethical.

Several times during the course of this book, we have touched on the question of the ethical. Already the fact that Kierkegaard recurrently writes about *the* ethical is worth noticing. Ethics is summarized in one specific attitude or point of view. This is especially seen in *Either/Or* where Kierkegaard (as we mentioned in chapter 3) writes about the category of ethics: the choice. The ethical seems to change meaning in Kierkegaard's later works. Kierkegaard indicates in *The Concept of Anxiety* that it is necessary to distinguish between meanings of the ethical. In the preface to the book, he distinguishes between what he calls the first and second ethics. First we need to understand what Kierkegaard means by second ethics, but before we even get that far, we must look at the different meanings of the ethical that we have touched on earlier in this book.

In *Either/Or* the concept of the ethical is defined as a stage or a life-view in opposition to the aesthetical. The ethicist, B, writes of the choice as his category; he specifies it in this way: it is the fundamental ethical choice between good and evil, but as that which creates the ethical aspect, it is the choice of this choice between good and evil. We must understand this to mean that in "the choice," the choice between good and evil is attributed a critical significance. The individual chooses himself since by choosing the choice he sees a critical significance in the ethical choice. He chooses himself as an individual who must choose and act ethically.

This seems to be a double-edged argument for the ethical. For it turns the ethical standpoint itself into a question of a choice; what is the basis for this choice of the ethical? B believes he can make a case for this standpoint against the alternative, the aesthetical indifference. His argument is that only the ethical choice provides continuity in the individual's life. It is only this choice that will prevent dispersion (*adspredthed*) in himself.

Choosing ourselves means, to the ethicist B, to repent, which again means to reconquer or appropriate our life that stretches back through the history of the human race. To choose ourselves is to discover that we are guilty, but it is precisely in this "taking possession of ourselves" that freedom lies. This is why B can link guilt and freedom, which on a first reading may look strange. However, this hinges on whether the movement of repentance is successful, which is what B presupposes. By fully repenting, the individual gains himself; he encounters himself as "posited" by himself. He has made himself his own.

However, it is worth noticing that B is faced with a blatant problem regarding this. To carry through with repentance is to gain transparency, but B mentions, at the same time, that man has a fundamental tendency not to want to be transparent to himself, and B evens links this tendency to hereditary sin.

First and Second Ethics

The Concept of Anxiety makes a radical shift at this point. The ethical is first of all determined as the task of becoming a whole individual, and each individual is faced with this task (117; 18-19), but then Kierkegaard distinguishes between the first and second ethics. The first ethics is characterized by the individual's striving to actualize the good as the ideal. This ethical striving, however, founders on the actuality of sin "with the aid of repentance" (116; 17). To conquer ourselves by way of repenting is impossible. The attempt to repent traps itself in anxiety about evil.

The second ethics has as its point of departure that with which the first ethics ends, the actuality of sin (118f; 20). The task that is the ethical (to become a "whole" or to become ourselves) is not annulled, but it cannot be actualized directly or continuously. The individual does not come forth to become "posited." The question is what is then implied by the second ethics. *The Concept of Anxiety* has little to say about this. Instead we must go to *Works of Love*, even if the term "the second ethics" is not used there. But before we do this, let us examine *Concluding Unscientific Postscript*.

In *Concluding Unscientific Postscript* the ethical is not only a stage or a life-view. The ethical is the task that the existing individual is faced with: to take over his existence. It is not a task we can choose to take or not take inasmuch as it belongs to being an individual. While in *Fear and Trembling*, the ethical is identical to the universal outside of which the single individual is placed, the ethical and existence are linked in *Concluding Unscientific Postscript* so that the ethical separates the single individual from "the others." But human existence that is defined by the ethical task is "marked" twice. It is marked a second time by the actuality of sin. How does this determine the ethical task?

In *Works of Love* the ethical demand is maintained at the same time that the individual, who must do the work of love, is understood as a dependant and already "posited" self. The individual is created with love as a fundamental impulse. His existence is carried by an already active love (Kierkegaard uses the expression that love is "present in the ground" [12, 210; 217]).

In what sense is this ethics? Kierkegaard maintains that the ethical distinguishes the single individual. The requirement is put before the single individual so as to reverse the perspective. We become a "You," the person addressed, since the requirement now means that we must manifest ourselves as the neighbor's neighbor. The requirement about loving "thy neighbor" is a duty, a universal requirement, but is the ethical still identical with the universal?

In the previous chapter I tried to show that Kierkegaard has another concept of the universal that, in fact, is ethical. It is a concept of the universal to which the religious exception is put in opposition. It is the universal as the universally human. This universally human is the basic ethical task that each individual is faced with and through which he becomes himself, this single individual. The task is the same for everyone ("*ligelig*") in the sense that it does not demand any particular armor or position. But the universally human also manifests itself in the requirement vis-à-vis the other person. For here the requirement means seeing the fundamental equality (*lighed*) or continuity with the other person. Thus, it is both the concept of the ethical as the fundamental requirement, which makes an individual a single individual, and the concept of the universally human as the universal likeness of all people, the fundamental human-equality or humanity (*menneske-lighed*)[1] that need to be

---

[1] See note 4 above. Trans.

addressed when we are to determine what is implied in the second ethics.

Self-love and Love Thy Neighbor

Several times in this book the ethical has been defined as the task of becoming ourselves. We may wonder why the task is supposed to be ethical and even *the* ethical. For surely the ethical only concerns the relation to the other person. The answer is that becoming ourselves does concern the other person, because becoming ourselves is to take over ourselves, to commit to ourselves, and this is the condition for ethical acts. Or rather, we take over ourselves by being committed to what we do.

We now have a second ethics that focuses ethics in the requirement of the relation to the other person, to our neighbor. That is to say that the other person stands immediately in an ethical relation to us and we may not even have chosen them ourselves. Kierkegaard distinguishes between the requirement to "love one's neighbor" and love as "preferential love" (12, 57; 53). When we have a preferential love for something, we have made a choice; we have selected something and not something else.

What happens with the self-relation when the ethical becomes the demand to "love one's neighbor"? As mentioned, the ethical demand distinguishes the single individual as he who must fulfill the demand. This is stressed with the demand to "love one's neighbor," since we do not only have another person before us; we have to manifest ourselves as the other's neighbor. Thus what we can call the ethical self-relation is maintained; we are still dealing with an ethical demand that the single individual commit (to) himself.

However, Kierkegaard further explores this relation between the demand in the relation to our neighbor and the self-relation. In fact he addresses the question about the relation between "love of one's neighbor" and self-love when he takes seriously the commandment that we must love our neighbor as ourselves.

First, Kierkegaard notices that the wording of the command-ment presupposes that an individual loves himself. But then he writes that an individual must learn how to love himself—and love himself the right way. What does this mean? Kierkegaard's answer is, "You shall love yourself in the same way as you love your neighbor when you love him as yourself" (12, 28; 23). This linguistically complicated statement reflects the fact that the relations (the relation to our neighbor and the self-relation) are intertwined. The requirement to "love one's neighbor" is not only determined by self-love ("as yourself"). The hidden requirement of loving ourselves is based on the requirement of "loving one's neighbor" ("in the same way as you love your neighbor"), which will be actualized when we love our neighbor as ourselves. The intertwining becomes an identification: "To love yourself in the right way and to love the neighbor correspond perfectly to one another; fundamentally they are one and the same thing" (ibid.; 22). The requirement is already a requirement for identification: you must love your neighbor *as* yourself (as though you were interacting with yourself). However, the question concerns the relation between relating to ourselves and relating to our neighbor. Love is identical in these two relations, but this identification occurs by mutually qualifying self-love and loving another person. We must love ourselves "*in the right way*" (ibid.).

Then what does it mean to love ourselves in the right way? Kierkegaard approaches the answer negatively. He describes phenomena in which we do not love ourselves, not in the right way in any case. The starting point is that the individual with some knowledge of people not only must have wished that he could encourage them to give up self-love, but he also must have wished just as strongly "that it were possible to teach them to love themselves" (12, 28; 23). But why do we need to learn what we automatically do, love ourselves? Kierkegaard's arguments are given in a series of descriptions that are worth quoting:

> When the bustler wastes his time and powers in the service of futile inconsequential pursuits, is this not because he has not learned rightly to love himself? When the light-minded person throws himself almost like a nonentity into the folly of the moment and makes nothing of it, is this not because he does not know how to love himself rightly? When the depressed person desires to be rid of life, indeed, of himself, is this not because he is unwilling to learn earnestly and rigorously to love himself? When someone surrenders to despair because the world or another person has faithlessly left him betrayed, what then is his fault (his innocent suffering is not referred to here) except not loving himself in the right way? When someone self-tormentingly thinks to do God a service by torturing himself, what is his sin except not willing to love himself in the right way? And if, alas, a person presumptuously lays violent hands upon himself, is not his sin precisely this, that he does not rightly love himself in the sense in which a person *ought* to love himself? (12, 28f; 23)

The descriptions depict an ascending line from the bustler, the light-minded person, to the depressed or despairing person and on to possibilities that seem to be the opposite: to torture oneself for God's sake or presumptuously (against God) to lay violent hands upon oneself. It is important to realize that the individual does something with himself in each of cases described in the passage. In this way the individual *surrenders* to despair. In all the described cases the point is self-abandonment. We give up on ourselves by wasting our lives doing something insignificant and futile (in the double sense of the word).[2] The light-minded person who "throws himself almost like a nonentity into the folly of the moment and makes nothing of it" gives up on himself by not taking himself seriously. That the line depicted in the descriptions is ascending is due to the fact that the self-abandonment becomes more and more distinct. It may be hard to understand that the busy person has given up on or abandoned himself; he is after all busy, maybe even with himself, but he avoids becoming aware of himself in busyness. The light-minded person thinks that the situation is not serious enough for us to speak of self-abandonment, which precisely is giving up on ourselves, abandoning ourselves. In the latter descriptions there is a more distinct wish to get rid of ourselves.

Thus we now know that self-abandonment is an obvious danger, and that it can be hard to love ourselves in the right way. But what does it mean to love ourselves in the right way? Here we must go to the complicated formulation of a previous passage: the right love of (one's) self runs parallel to the love for our neighbor. But how? At the end of the chapter from which I have been quoting, the subject concerns to sorrow:

I do not have the right to become insensitive to life's pain, because I *shall* sorrow; but neither do I have the right to despair, because I *shall* sorrow; and neither do I have the right to stop sorrowing, because I *shall* sorrow.

---

[2] In Danish, *forfængelig* has a double meaning that is lost in English. *Forfængelig* means both futile and being self-absorbed. Trans.

So it is with love. You do not have the right to become insensitive to this feeling, because you *shall* love; but neither do you have the right to love despairingly, because you *shall* love; and just as little do you have the right to warp this feeling in you, because you *shall* love. You shall preserve love, and you shall preserve yourself and by and in preserving yourself preserve love. (12, 47f; 43)

To harden ourselves against "life's pain" that we feel or against the love we feel is, as I indicated in chapter 5, to lose ourselves in such a way that we wound our souls. We do something with ourselves; we harden ourselves against our feelings. It is worth noticing that the feeling of love is already in us and that we can harden ourselves against it. Love, as well as sorrow, can become despair; or rather, we can love in·despair while sorrow can become despair, but if sorrow becomes despair we give up grieving in a certain way. The despair turns to ourselves because we have given up hope. When we feel sorrow, we must sorrow in order to avoid despairing.

Indirectly, Kierkegaard is distinguishing between hardening oneself and despairing. When we harden ourselves against our own feelings, we become unmoved. The person in despair (he who feels *himself* in despair) is affected or moved by himself. In both cases the point is self-abandonment; we lose ourselves, but we lose ourselves in two different ways: in the first case we lose ourselves in such a way that we do not feel ourselves; in the second case we lose ourselves by being beside ourselves.

We were seeking an answer to the question about what it means to love ourselves in the right way. In the quoted passage it states that we must preserve ourselves, and we must do this by preserving love. To preserve ourselves means not to give up on ourselves. We were just shown that not loving ourselves in the right way means giving up on ourselves in different ways. Kierkegaard states that it is a duty to love ourselves that we must understand this way: you are not allowed to give up on yourself. This self-love in which we preserve ourselves in a way against ourselves runs parallel to the love of our neighbor, as previously mentioned. The self-love does this because we are left to receiving and accepting ourselves. We must receive ourselves as we receive the other person. But self-love not only makes a detour around the relation to the other person; it is preserved only by and through the love of our neighbor. This finds its reason in the fact that freedom as self-agreement belongs to self-devotion, according to Kierkegaard. We become free in the love that is given us as a gift more than it is our own achievement. This is what the second ethics emphasizes, and by emphasizing this, it maintains that the ethical means to become ourselves. In order to become free in love, we must "go through" the anxiety for the possibility of change that is implied in the spontaneous love. This is what occurs, according to Kierkegaard, when the spontaneous love itself changes by the requirement to "love one's neighbor" as yourself. Self-relation and the relation to the other person are entangled in such a way that, to use the words in *The Concept of Anxiety*, in "communication" a "continuity" manifests itself, which is a continuity with oneself as well as with the other person.

CHAPTER 9

Faith

The Religious

As previous chapters show, the relation between the ethical and the religious is complicated. In *Either/Or* the ethical and the religious are put together in such a way that the religious is reduced to being a support for the ethical. However, in *Fear and Trembling* the religious is what suspends the ethical; here the ethical is reduced. In *Concluding Unscientific Postscript* the ethical functions as the constituting factor for human existence, and the religious functions as a second "marking" of this existence in relation to the ethical as the first "marking." By the second accentuation of subjectivity as (un)truth, the religious provides us with a new starting point. When *The Concept of Anxiety* speaks of a first and second ethics, what is crucial to understand is that the ethical itself has been determined by this new starting point. It has been qualified religiously.

We can debate the meaning of the relation between the ethical and the religious. Is the point that it is necessary to go through the ethical in order to get to the religious? If so, there is also the reverse point that the ethical itself is transcended and in this movement it is, at the same time, qualified. In addition, it is important that the religious itself, as much as "the aesthetical" and "the ethical," is not unequivocal. On the contrary, we find the point in how the religious is further determined. The "Christian-religious" (10, 136; 451) is distinguished from the "merely" religious precisely by the accentuation of existence and the ethical as existence "marked" for the second time, as a second ethics.

The Relation to God

Kierkegaard determines the religious by the relation to God, but just as the religious is understood in different ways, so also is the relation to God. It is, nonetheless, possible to find an assertion that is the basis for all the different ways of understanding the relation to God. This assertion is hidden in a passage that I have already quoted from or rather in one single sentence that I left out of my passage. I am referring to the description of what it means to become ourselves in *Sickness unto Death*. As we saw earlier, the passage begins like this: "The self is the conscious synthesis of infinitude and finitude that relates itself to itself, whose task is to become itself"; it continues like this: "which can be done only through the relationship to God" (15, 87; 29-30).

The passage refers to the beginning of *Sickness unto Death* where man is determined as a self and where the self is determined as a relation relating to itself. But "such a relation that relates itself to itself, a self, must either have established itself or have been established by another" (15, 73; 13). Then Kierkegaard starts arguing for the latter: the self has been established by "another," which means other than itself. "The human self is such a derived, established relation" (15, 73; 13). In other words, the self is a derived or dependant relation, since it is a relation to that which has established the relation. By relating to itself, the self is relating to this "other."

Until now it seems that the passage only states that man as a self has been established by another since the self has not established itself; but Kierkegaard also gives us an argument for why it has not established itself. The argument proceeds from the fact that there are two kinds of despair in the strict sense: in despair not to will to be oneself and in despair to will to be oneself. If man had been established by himself (i.e., had himself in his own power), there would only be one form of despair: "not to will to be oneself, to will to do away with oneself, but there could not be the form: in despair to will to be oneself" (ibid.; 14). In despair to will to be oneself is exactly wanting to have ourselves in our own power, determining for ourselves who we are. This despair shows that we are already determined as something specific and as something other than what we want ourselves to be.

Sickness unto Death wishes to prove further that man has not been established by himself. But, put positively, man is an "established," dependant relation in the sense that he is already placed in relation to himself as a particular self. This must be proved by examining the despair where an individual in despair does not want to will to be himself as this particular self. When man in this way tries to "establish himself," the self-relation becomes a misrelation because man has already been "established"; he is already a particular self.

Thus the basic argument is that man, by relating to himself, relates to God. Everything depends on whether this is correctly understood. God is "other" than the self in the sense that God is the one who established the self, and in this way the self maintains that it is this particular self.

Some may believe that this is a rather abstract concept of God. For the ethicist in *Either/Or*, God is the authority in relation to whom the ethicist places himself vis-à-vis his choice of himself. Also in *Sickness unto Death* God is the "authority," the eternal, that holds an individual firmly to himself. God is the "criterion" (*Maalestokken*) for the self, which means, "that directly before which it is a self" (15, 133; 79). However, more is implied in what *Sickness unto Death* states about the relation to God.

Firstly, the relation to God is defined by conscience (15, 173; 124): "God pays attention to one" (15, 123; 69). In *Works of Love* Kierkegaard explicitly states that "the relationship between the individual and God, the God-relationship, is the conscience" (12, 140; 143). Secondly, the individual at issue here is not in a safeguarded situation. It may be that he is trying to make it look as if he is, but safeguarding oneself is now claimed to be nothing other than despair. We are caught no matter how we twist and turn the situation; what is essential here is that the individual understands this himself. The situation is anything but safeguarded, for, in fact, we do not have anything to hold on to which the individual realizes by having an uneasy conscience.

The God of *Sickness unto Death* (or rather the God of the first half of the book) is a God who has created and preserves man. This is also manifested in a situation where an individual can no longer see any possibilities before him. God is here determined as the one for whom there is always a possibility. Consequently, God is placed outside of any human yardstick. This is repeated in that God is also the one who redeems an individual from himself, from the imprisonment to which he ties himself. Thus we are getting close to what was stated in *The Concept of Anxiety* where the good (which anxiety about the good turns against) was, in the last analysis, conceived as "the word" (207; 124) that redeems from the outside and restores freedom. We have reached what Kierkegaard calls the "Christian-religious." God redeems man of sin (sin understood as the unfreedom to which the individual ties himself). But, as has already been shown, sin is not unambiguous. *Philosophical Fragments* defines sin as the untruth and unfreedom that an individual is in by his own doing; but that man is a sinner is also distinctly defined by his relation to God. In part 3 of *Upbuilding Discourses in Various Spirits*, it states, "The fundamental relation between God and a human being is that a human being is a sinner and God is the Holy One. Directly before God a human being is not a sinner in this or in that, but is essentially a sinner, is not guilty of this or that, but is essentially and unconditionally guilty" (11, 264; 285). The passage needs an explanation, for how can man be guilty if he cannot be blamed for something specifically? That an individual is basically or always guilty is explained by Kierkegaard when he states that any direct accounting between man and God is impossible. This must be explained by the mode of thought we saw developed in *Works of Love* where God's act comes first. An individual begins by being in debt to love, even in the sense that he is himself given the incitement of love and does not himself create the love that he feels. No matter how much he pays back his debt, he can never fully pay it back.

We started this section with Kierkegaard's assertion that an individual, in relating to himself, relates to God. Thus self-relation is a self-relation by implying a relation to God. However, it can be difficult to comprehend how the conclusions we have reached so far are a result of the self-relation, for instance that God is the one for whom everything is possible. Kierkegaard emphasizes that we only realize this rightly when we see ourselves without any possibilities; we can then ask if, in this situation, it is not more obvious to maintain that we actually find ourselves in a hopeless situation. This is, in fact, also what Kierkegaard states. For to realize that to God everything is possible is to believe and to believe that which is unlikely and even unreasonable.

Anxiety and Faith

Chapter 5, which ends *The Concept of Anxiety*, carries the title "Anxiety as Saving through Faith." We must understand the title this way: faith saves us from the anxiety that makes us unfree. We could therefore reasonably expect that all the loose ends will be tied up towards the end of the book, and that Kierkegaard will provide an answer towards which the four previous chapters pointed. But almost the opposite occurs. I took a long detour, primarily through *Sickness unto Death*, because the final chapter of *The Concept of Anxiety* is disappointing by not giving much information on the relation to God and faith.

The question is whether anxiety is annulled in faith. Insofar as faith should be the answer to the anxiety that makes us unfree, the answer seems to be "yes." But faith saves through anxiety, or rather anxiety saves through faith. What does this mean? What role does anxiety have in this situation?

The meaning of anxiety that we are dealing with in the final chapter of *The Concept of Anxiety* is anxiety as the possibility of freedom, or to put it more precisely, it is anxiety that anticipates the possibility. When we feel comfortable or safeguarded in our lives, anxiety anticipates the possibility that we can lose that on which this life depends. Anxiety anticipates the possibility of loss. In anxiety we can therefore see through what we otherwise stop at, but where does the look of anxiety stop? What do we have to hold on to?

The role anxiety plays here is that of evoking a threatening nothingness, and how can nothingness save or make us free? What we need to examine is that anxiety not only anticipates and therefore evokes nothingness; it is also educative. Anxiety is even educative by bringing out the threat of nothingness. The point is this: an individual can be absorbed by the circumstances in his life, and maybe even by the things with which he surrounds himself. Thus the individual must learn not to identify himself with the "finite relations" of life that are mutable. In anxiety the individual breaks loose from what he otherwise can be absorbed by or lose himself in. In other words, the individual learns in anxiety that he is something other than what he identifies himself with.

But we have also seen that the task is to take the specific circumstances of our lives on ourselves. Anxiety seems to provide what we previously called "separation," namely separation from the world. And this separation was temporary; its aim was to return from the world to confirm that we are an inseparable part of our world. But the question is if the movement in anxiety is not pushed even further. Do we return to what we in anxiety broke loose from? What stops anxiety?

In the final chapter of *The Concept of Anxiety*, anxiety anticipates the possibility of loss to such a degree that the possibility seems to disappear. It is the loss of all. "But whoever took possibility's course in misfortune lost all, all, as no one in actuality ever lost it" (237; 158). But he also retrieves everything if he did "not defraud the possibility that wanted to teach him and did not wheedle the anxiety that wanted to save him" (ibid.; 158). That is to say, if anxiety has its full effect. But how would he retrieve everything? Here we can return to the expression "through faith." Anxiety only saves through faith, and even though Kierkegaard does not explore faith further, faith must mean that it is God who gives back to man what he has lost.

Anxiety can therefore lead an individual to faith. It can do this since it "anxiously torments everything finite and petty" out of the individual (ibid.; 159). This also means that "the individual through anxiety is educated unto faith" (238; 159). The education to which Kierkegaard is referring is not the education of his age that he otherwise ridicules. His own age speaks of education to distinguish between "the educated" and the common man. Education in this case is based on views about what is wise to do and what we should do when we belong to the educated class. But anxiety consumes the common views and calculations of wisdom. When anxiety is educative, we have "possibility's course in misfortune" where we lose our footing in this common world. Anxiety frees the individual in a sense. In a passage in *Fear and Trembling*, Kierkegaard asks, "What, then, is education?" His answer is, "I believed it is the course the individual goes through in order to catch up with himself, and the person who will not go through this course is not much helped by being born in the most enlightened age" (5, 44; 46).

The education of anxiety is possibility's course that each individual must take. In anxiety we learn that we are guilty, but not guilty in any finite sense, guilty of a specific thing. We are "infinitely guilty" (239; 161). But "he who in relation to guilt is educated by anxiety will rest only in the Atonement" (240; 162). Thus *The Concept of Anxiety* ends abruptly.

It is not a simple matter to explain the relation between anxiety and faith that is implied in the title of the final chapter of *The Concept of Anxiety*. Anxiety is supposed to lead to faith, which is supposed to annul anxiety. But faith can only do this by a leap out of anxiety. Anxiety can be misunderstood so that it does not lead us to faith but away from faith. Kierkegaard even adds that to the individual, anxiety will be "a serving spirit that against its will leads him where he wishes to go" (237; 159) to the individual. So, anxiety does not automatically lead us to faith. Anxiety can save—through faith.

Even though anxiety in this way seems to be subordinated to faith, anxiety is necessary to get to faith. What is important is to take anxiety on ourselves and even to take its course. We only become free of anxiety by first going through anxiety, and not just the anxiety that can appear every now and then, but the anxiety of possible. "Only he who passes through the anxiety of the possible is educated to have no anxiety" (236; 157).

But are we then free of anxiety in faith? An earlier passage in *The Concept of Anxiety* states that only faith is able "to renounce anxiety without anxiety"—"faith does not thereby annihilate anxiety, but, itself eternally young, it extricates itself from anxiety's moment of death" (201; 117). If we maintain that anxiety concerns the possibility, has a sense of its ambiguity, the next question is then if faith comes with an anxiety, namely an anxiety that is a paradoxical possibility. We can here go from *The Concept of Anxiety* back to *Fear and Trembling* in which Kierkegaard discusses "the distress and anxiety in the paradox of faith" (5, 69; 75). In *Fear and Trembling* a connection is made between faith as "a task for a whole lifetime" and anxiety "that no man outgrows" and that the heart must be young enough not to forget (5, 10; 7).

The Decision of Faith

The paradoxical possibility that I touched on is described in *Fear and Trembling* as the absurd: the possibility of getting "everything" back that was lost. But, as we saw, faith not only relates to the situation where what we cling to is lost. Faith also relates to our anxious discovery of being infinitely guilty. The paradoxical possibility becomes a possibility of redemption from the guilt from which we cannot free ourselves.

Faith as faith in the paradox is what Kierkegaard calls faith in the eminent sense. The paradox is the incarnation, i.e., that God became man. That this is a paradox means that it contains contradictory elements. The paradox is that God, the eternal, has been incarnated in history as an individual. This stands in contrast to our conception of God as eternal. "That the by-nature eternal comes into existence in time, is born, grows up, and dies is a break with all thinking" (10, 245; 579). Faith in the paradox is a faith of "the most improbable" (6, 50; 52).

Since faith cannot rest on what we normally cling to but is a faith despite what we regard as probable, faith becomes the individual's decision. Since it is a decision against "all thinking," it seems to be a blind decision. Kierkegaard suggests this when, for instance, he states that "faith begins precisely where thought stops" (5, 50; 53). Or when he states that "right here is faith's struggle: to believe without being able to understand" (11, 253; 273). Nevertheless, the paradox needs to be understood. It is necessary to understand *that* it is the paradox and not just something meaningless.

The understanding that the paradox asks for does not stop here, for we need to understand what the paradox means. That God becomes man, takes on human form, means that God moves to meet man. This has a double sense, for this "moving to meet man" is redemption, but man as a sinner is, at the same time, the one who needs to be redeemed. The paradox is not abstract but has a crucial meaning through which human existence manifests itself as "marked" and defined anew. Thus the individual who faces the paradox must not only understand that it is a paradox, but he also must understand how crucial the paradox is.

This does not annul what is contradictory about the paradox, but it is important to realize what the paradox is contrary to. Kierkegaard often states that it is the understanding, but the understanding means man's attempt to control his existence (*tilværelse*) through wisdom and calculation. The paradox is contradictory by turning upside down the ideas and expectations according to which people normally organize their lives, for instance, the relationship between weakness and strength, power and powerlessness, poverty and wealth, low and high status, or losing and winning. Faith must contain an understanding of this contradiction or the reevaluation of our conceptions.

When Kierkegaard emphasizes faith as the utter decision where the single individual has nothing to cling to and where he therefore can only stand alone, he is arguing with the tendency of his own time to turn Christianity into something we automatically belong to by being born into a Christian culture. Faith is the individual's decision—to choose himself.

The Equality of the Eternal

Before we examine Kierkegaard's diagnosis of his own time, we must once again go to his analysis of the God-relationship. As previously mentioned, the assertion in *Sickness unto Death* is that an individual in his relation to himself is also in a relation to God. The situation was that a human being as a relation has either established himself or has been established by another. Since the self-relation proves to be a specific relation when an individual seeks to determine himself, Kierkegaard believes that he can exclude the first possibility that a human being has established himself.

However, faith does not come automatically. On the contrary, faith is a daring venture. That God is something totally different that falls outside of any human yardstick means that God has no characteristics. But if there are no characteristics, how can Kierkegaard then determine the difference between God and man? He poses the question in *Philosophical Fragments* and adds a further comment: "But this difference cannot be grasped securely. Every time this happens, it is basically an arbitrariness, and at the very bottom of devoutness there madly lurks the capricious arbitrariness that knows it itself has produced the god" (6, 45; 45).

If the conception of God is man-made, it is natural to understand the other (in relation to which a human being is a self) as other people or humanity in general. Kierkegaard touches on this possibility implicitly, since he tries to explain the meaning of the God-relationship. The point of departure is that social relations between people can become stunted by the individuals' evaluation of and comparison to each other. The mutual differences are the occasion for such an evaluation, for instance the difference in social position. The solidarity can even depend on an evaluation that excludes certain other people. If there is no other authority, the individual in the evaluation of himself is left to the common evaluation that prevails. In contrast to this, Kierkegaard proposes what he calls "the equality of the eternal": that every individual is a single individual vis-à-vis God. This means that the single individual escapes others in the mutual relationship. This is so by virtue of the fundamental equality where each individual is posed in the same way: as an individual. The equality of the eternal means, therefore, a universal likeness of all people, a human-equality or humanity (*menneske-lighed*) that precedes and can be contrary to the mutual evaluations that mark important changes. The requirement is that each individual must "become free, independent, oneself" (12, 267; 278). This is a theme that can be found in many other contexts in Kierkegaard's writings. "There are people who have inhumanly forgotten that everyone should fortify himself by means of the universal divine likeness of all people, have forgotten that therefore, whether a person is man or woman, poorly or richly endowed, master or slave, beggar or plutocrat, the relationships among human beings ought and may never be such that the one worships and the other is the one worshiped" (12, 124; 125). Thus Kierkegaard's assertion is that the fundamental of human-equality or humanity (*menneske-lighed*) is deeply rooted in the God-relationship by virtue of which each individual is distinguished as an individual.

In the preface of the work "The Single Individual," to which I have previously referred, Kierkegaard simply states that "the essentially religious is the true humanity /menneskelighed/" (18, 150; 104). His argument is that the secular sphere that is defined by peoples' doings (*gøre-mål*) for and against each other, by what they have for or against each other, is invariably defined by the difference that they use as a cause to create differences. The religious can be the true likeness of all people or humanity (*menneske-lighed*) by being deprived of this secular sphere. The religious provides a last perspective that, as such, is a perspective on what people do; it is not a perspective outside which we, with all our doings, can place ourselves.

According to Kierkegaard, such a final perspective means an ultimate hope. In a passage in *Upbuilding Discourses in Various Spirits*, Kierkegaard writes about "hope that there is a resurrection where there will be no differences, where the deaf will hear, the blind will see, the one who was miserably shaped will be as beautiful as everyone else" (11, 104; 111).

CHAPTER 10

"Our Time"

When Kierkegaard in *Concluding Unscientific Postscript* emphasizes what seems obvious, i.e., that an individual is existing, and thus puts a special emphasis on the concept of existence, he is, as shown in chapter 2, in opposition to the forgetfulness of his own time. The recurrent formula is that "in our time" we have forgotten what existence and inwardness mean. Kierkegaard also speaks of "in our time, when inwardness has been completely forgotten" (113 fn; 14 fn), in *The Concept of Anxiety*.

The expression "our time" appears time and time again in Kierkegaard's writings. As a rule, it is not identified with something good. Even though the critical diagnosis of "our time" is not as central in *The Concept of Anxiety* as in his later works, the book does provide a key concept of this diagnosis: spiritlessness. This proves once again how *The Concept of Anxiety* opens the door to the other books by virtue of the meaning that is attributed to anxiety.

Several times in this book we have touched on the complex relations that Kierkegaard summarizes in the word *spiritlessness*. On a first reading, spiritlessness means absence or lack of spirit, but Kierkegaard distinguishes between an absence of spirit in the strict sense and spiritlessness. With spiritlessness we speak of a loss. Spiritlessness is when we are not aware of ourselves as spirit or self, according to Kierkegaard. How can we then speak of loss? First of all, by man being a spirit or self in such a way that he relates to himself and others. We are in this way, which is precisely what the analysis of anxiety reveals, situated under the determination of becoming a spirit or self in the accentuated sense that we strive to become aware of ourselves and to pull ourselves together from "dispersion" and "grow" together with ourselves. Second, we can speak of a loss in the sense that we are not just unaware of being a self. An individual can hide this fact from himself, as the analysis of anxiety has revealed. The self-relation can be evaded or covered up at the same time as this evasion or cover-up demands a self-relation. Spiritlessness designates a particularly complex phenomenon: that the loss of self is not made into something special.[1] This can precisely happen by adjusting ourselves or making ourselves "as courant /passable/ as a circulating coin," as it is stated in *Sickness unto Death* (15, 91; 34). One tries to make it inconspicuous that one is not "oneself." It is this possibility of hiding despair from ourselves that is implied when Kierkegaard calls despair ordinary. As we have shown, the lurking anxiety reveals that what is at issue is despair.

Speaking of the "generality" of despair and anxiety already opens up a kind of social diagnosis or description of different forms of social life. This is supported by the fact that Kierkegaard often names the form that spiritlessness assumes since he speaks of the philistine-bourgeois person. Since spiritlessness succeeds by virtue of a way of relating to other people (namely by adjusting to the way we regard "other people," which again will determine the way we regard ourselves), it is natural to use the concept in a social diagnosis.

Kierkegaard's diagnosis of his own time does not fully blossom until *A Literary Review*, which was published in March 1846 just after *Concluding Unscientific Postscript*. In a review of Thomasine Gyllembourg's short story *Two Ages*, Kierkegaard

---

[1] Arne Grøn uses the word *umærkeligt* to play on *mærke* (mark or feel) or *mærkelig* (strange). Also see note 16 above. Trans.

puts "the present age" (14, 63; 68) up against "the age of revolution" (1790s) (14, 57; 61). While "the age of revolution" is essentially passionate, "the present age" is passionless since it is influenced by calculations of prudence.

This common sense is a social circumstance. In a passionate era, enthusiasm is the principle that unites; in an era without passion, envy becomes the principle that negatively unites the different individuals. Once the comparison of envy has been established, envy becomes *leveling* (14, 77; 84). Kierkegaard defines *leveling* in the strict sense as "the public" (14, 86; 93), which is a result of "the abstraction of 'the press'" and "the passionlessness...of the age" (14, 86; 93). The public is "an all encompassing something that is nothing" (14, 83; 90). When the public has an opinion about something, it is no one in particular who has this opinion. Even though the public is an abstraction, the concept has a reality that is an all-encompassing something.

Leveling means total anonymity: the individual becomes one more number in a mass. Leveling comes about because of the social sphere, that is, by a negative principle of solidarity. Even though it is an abstract power that manifests itself, it only works by the way the individual views himself and other people. The individuals turn themselves into a mass. Leveling means that the relation between people changes. When individuals lack inwardness, the relation between them is actually not a relation since they are not connected positively. "The opposites do not relate to each other but stand, as it were, and carefully watch each other, *and this tension is actually the termination of the relation*" (14, 72; 78).

Kierkegaard describes different phenomena in which leveling manifests itself. For instance, "chattering" means that the passionate difference between being silent and speaking disappears. A real conversation presupposes that the single individual can be silent "essentially," whereas "chatter just continues" (now about one thing, now about another) without difference. The separation between the private and the public in "a private-public garrulousness, which is just about what the public is" (14, 91; 100), is abolished by this chatter. The public sphere degenerates qua a public.

With this analysis, Kierkegaard believes that he has given a description of what negatively distinguishes "the present age." But he indicates that here we also must go through the negative. By its abstract unification the present age also provides an opportunity: that the individual is "educated" through this abstraction to regain himself. It is not until this occurs that a unification in the strict sense is possible: "Not until the single individual has established an ethical stance despite the whole world, not until then can there be any question of genuinely uniting" (14, 97; 106). Thus the social is not made an antithesis to the individual. Even though leveling comes about through the social, it is the individuals who turn themselves into a mass. The way out of leveling is the single individual's separation, but in this way he gains the true universal that unites the individuals positively.

When Kierkegaard describes the public as "an all encompassing something that is nothing," he has turned anxiety inside out. Leveling produces the opposite movement of the separation of anxiety in which the individual becomes a single individual. To be sure, Kierkegaard asserts that the all-consuming leveling can become educative as is anxiety, but it is only so by virtue of a separation that itself presupposes anxiety as the possibility of freedom. What works in leveling is a kind of anxiety of spiritlessness. Even though Kierkegaard does not explicitly mention anxiety or spiritlessness in *A Literary Review*, the connection is obvious.

The concept of spiritlessness was framed in the historic-philosophical outline that Kierkegaard worked out in *The Concept of Anxiety*. As was shown, spiritlessness is a possibility within Christianity. Since Christianity points out that man is spirit, it is also possible to lose this understanding. That man is spirit also means that each individual is a self in such a way that he is a single individual. Kierkegaard speaks of "our modern age" (14, 82; 90) in *A Literary Review*. Spiritlessness understood as losing the consciousness of being a single individual takes the form of leveling in *A Literary Review*, and leveling is possible by virtue of the fact that our modern age liberates new possibilities. In a way this was already indicated in *Concluding Unscientific Postscript*. In Kierkegaard's book, it was stated that the present age is characterized by an accumulation of knowledge that enables us to forget another knowledge: that which each individual knows "primitively," within himself, when he is aware of himself. The ethical knowledge as a knowledge about ourselves in relation to others is a knowledge that the single individual holds "within himself."

Kierkegaard almost anticipates that in modern society a dramatic increase of possibilities for communication will take place. In *A Literary Review* he notes this irony: "The velocity of the transportation system and the speed of communication stand in an inverse relationship to the dilatoriness of irresolution" (14, 59; 64). The more "communication" we have, the more suffocating the possibility of the power of comparison becomes. The individual forgets himself as a single individual in the negative mutuality of comparison.

In *Sickness unto Death*, which was published in 1849, Kierkegaard not only speaks of spiritlessness but of "the anxiety that characterizes spiritlessness." Just prior to this passage Kierkegaard refers to *The Concept of Anxiety* (15, 100; 44).

However, Kierkegaard stated in *The Concept of Anxiety* that "in spiritlessness there is no anxiety, because it is too happy, too content, and too spiritless for that" (182; 95). But already on the next page he asserts that anxiety, nonetheless, is within spiritlessness, and at the end of *The Concept of Anxiety* he hints at the opinion that is articulated in *Sickness unto Death*: if an individual prides himself on never being in anxiety, the answer is that only the person who has gone through the possibility of anxiety is educated not to be in anxiety. "If, on the other hand, the speaker maintains that the great thing about him is that he has never been in anxiety, I will gladly provide him with my explanation: that it is because he is very spiritless" (236; 157). It is natural to take one further step in the explanation: "The anxiety that characterizes spiritlessness is recognized precisely by its spiritless sense of security" (15, 100; 44).

Spiritlessness consists in a complex self-relation where the individual makes the loss of self (which is despair) inconspicuous to himself. In this way spiritlessness confirms the self-relation that it also tries to evade. This ambiguous self-relation is the anxiety of spiritlessness. "Nevertheless, anxiety lies underneath" (ibid.; 44). Anxiety is present as an underlying restlessness that makes it evident that we are dealing with despair. Anxiety does not have to manifest itself openly so that we become aware of it as anxiety. It can manifest itself in the way in which it conceals itself as anxiety, namely in a restlessness or insecurity in the midst of tranquility or safety. Already the fact that we must safeguard ourselves reveals anxiety. And this can be revealed in language. We can, using an expression from the final chapter of *The Concept of Anxiety*, try to "wheedle" anxiety (237; 158). We calm ourselves not only vis-à-vis other people (how we talk about ourselves), but also by becoming one of "the others" (where we talk the way other people talk).

Fundamentally the meaning of anxiety reveals that an individual is a self. Anxiety as the possibility of freedom is the possibility of becoming aware of ourselves. Spiritlessness is the counterpoint. It is the possibility of becoming unaware of ourselves; a possibility that we have ourselves, but a part of this counter pointed possibility is in anxiety. For the meaning of anxiety is, as was shown, ambiguous: it is the possibility of discovering ourselves, but it is also an ambiguous way of relating. In anxiety we can enclose ourselves on ourselves (the demonic enclosing reserve) or try to evade anxiety (spiritlessness). That we speak of anxiety even in the latter case shows, by contrast, that the possibility of freedom is present as the possibility we evade.

"No period, no age, and therefore not the present one, either, can halt the skepticism of leveling," Kierkegaard writes in *A Literary Review*. And he adds, "It can be halted only if the individual, an individual separateness, gains the intrepidity of religiousness" (14, 79; 86), which may sound like an impotent protest since leveling (and Kierkegaard emphasizes this himself) is an abstract power that plays its tricks with individuals. But since leveling begins with what the single individual does with himself in his relation to other people, the change also begins here. The individual gains intrepidity by not fearing what no man must fear (i.e., other people, which is the power of comparison), but by fearing what every man must fear (i.e., himself, which is conscience). The counterpart to leveling is the separation of anxiety in which the single individual becomes aware of himself—as a self. This is what Kierkegaard calls gaining an "essential" humanity, since the individual "does not inhumanely confuse himself with some abstract something, with the times, our age, etc., but in and through his own proper grasp of what it is to be a human being" (14, 102; 112). An individual is taught this by being separated—by learning to be anxious.

It is precisely the ambiguous possibility, which is a part of anxiety, that reveals that it is critical to learn how to be in anxiety. For what is implied in this is to be anxious the right way.

Suggestions for Further Reading

If one desires to keep up to date with the fast-growing literature on Kierkegaard, I can recommend the journal *Kierkegaardiana* that comes out once a year. Aside from articles on Kierkegaard, *Kierkegaardiana* consists of reviews of books on Kierkegaard and a yearly bibliography on the literature on Kierkegaard by Aage Jørgensen.

The interpretation I have presented in this book has first and foremost been inspired by a small but not easily read book by Michael Theunissen: *Das Selbst auf dem Grund der Verzweiflung. Kierkegaard's negativistische Methode* (Frankfurt am Main, 1991), published in English in October 2003. Theunissen proposes the thesis that Kierkegaard in *Sickness unto Death* presupposes the negative, despair, when he is to explain what the self is, and not the other way around. Theunissen's article "Kierkegaard's Negativistic Method" in *Psychiatry and the Humanities, Vol. 5: Kierkegaard's Truth: The Disclosure of the Self*, ed. William Kerrigan and Joseph H. Smith (New Haven CT: Yale University Press, 1981, pp. 381–423) is also recommended.

Among the Danish literature on Kierkegaard available in English, I must point out one extraordinary book, Kresten Nordentoft's *Kierkegaard's Psychology*, translated by Bruce Kirmmse (Pittsburgh: Duquesne University Press, 1978, vol. 7 of Duquesne Studies—Psychological Studies).

For a variety of perspectives on Kierkegaard's *The Concept of Anxiety*, I recommend the excellent book *The Concept of Anxiety, International Kierkegaard Commentary*, vol. 8, ed. Robert L. Perkins (Macon GA: Mercer University Press, 1985).

Also suggested:

Ferreira, M. Jamie, *Kierkegaard*. Blackwell, 2008.

Hannay, Alastair & Marino, Gordon, ed., *The Cambridge Companion to Kierkegaard*. Cambridge: Cambridge University Press, 1998.

Kirmmse, Bruce H., *Kierkegaard in Golden Age Denmark*. Bloomington IN: Indiana University Press, 1990.

Pattison, George, *The Philosophy of Søren Kierkegaard*, Chesham: Acumen, 2005.

Theunissen, Michael, *Kierkegaard's Concept of Despair*, trans. B. Harshav and H. Illbruck. Princeton: Princeton University Press, 2005.

Westphal, Merold, *Becoming a Self: A Reading of Kierkegaard's Concluding Unscientific Postscript*. West Lafayette IN: Purdue University Press, 1996.